Here's what 1
Pow(

MW01614726

"Human beings have enormous potential and Power Performance offers an exciting new way for everyone to tap into that potential. Just think how it would feel to always have the power to be your best and really believe that you CAN follow your dreams. This book offers easy, simple and fun ways to change the way you program your brain, and achieve anything you desire."
— Dr. Joe Vitale, author of *The Attractor Factor*, www.mrfire.com

"No matter what field a person is in, true genius is the ability to reduce a seemingly complicated world to its actual simplicity. We are all capable of that, and through this book Carrol has given us all the power of achievement. Through management I have seen her energy, talent and personality shared with thousands of concert goers, and what a gift to now go way beyond these parameters to share her gifts with each and every one of us."
— Bob Kay, Partner, Concert Productions, LLC,
Former Vice President, Columbia Artists Management

"Dr. Carrol's Power Performance is full of dynamic and stimulating techniques to help overcome insecurities and fears whether in music performance or any life's stressful situations. I highly recommend it!"
— Susann McDonald, Dinstinguished Prof. of Music, Indiana
University, Artistic Director, World Harp Congress

"Internationally renowned harpist and educator, Carrol McLaughlin, graces us with her timeless knowledge in this outstanding book. Whether you are a highly successful performer, a multi-disciplined lawyer or a stay at home parent under constant pressure, this book is an essential tool in mastering the performance that affects every element of your daily life."
— Dr. Ernst J. Walch, Internationl Lawyer

"Dr. Carrol has brought together, and presented in a clearly understandable way, many strategies for outstanding performances by anyone. From school children memorizing math facts or spelling words, to adults giving a lecture or business training seminar, the practices described here will assist the individual in achieving the desired outcomes. Neuro Linguistic Programming is based on sound principles that have been shown to work over and over again. In the best of all worlds, every teacher and parent would learn and teach these strategies to their children and students. What a difference it could make!"
— Dr. Margaret Dunlap, PhD, Retired School Psychologist

"Dr. Carrol McLaughlin is truly one of the most positive people I have ever met. With her magnificent influence, Dr. McLaughlin has created a new and amazing book, "Power Performance". I love her cutting edge techniques which inspire, teach and challenge. Buy it. Don't skim through it or borrow it. You're going to

want your own copy. I will refer to these phenomenal techniques again and again as I teach and perform."
— Julie Gaisford Keyes, Harpist, Mormon Tabernacle Choir,
Professional Harpist and Teacher, Salt Lake City

"I had the honor to meet Dr. Carrol when I attended the most wonderful concert I have ever seen, as she performed at the Cairo Opera House. I admire her as a person, teacher, classical musician, jazz musician and composer for harp. She has a wonderful positive energy which she shares always with her students and other people. Dr. Carrol has a deep understanding of the stage and the necessary preparation for a successful performance. In her book she shares with us her personal experiences of performances around the world, mixed with the expert study of Neuro Linguistic Programming. Thanks for this book!"
— Yasser El Serafi, First Concertmaster,
Cairo Symphony Orchestra

"The ultimate performance guide! Every performer should utilize the wonderful ideas contained in this book. It is perfect for speakers, actors, and musicians alike. I use these techniques daily."
—Dr. Cathryn Clayton, Professor of Harp, University of Utah

"Power Performance is a very much needed self-help text book for anybody who wants to perform better regardless of their profession. It gives invaluable advice for performing musicians and makes us all understand that we 'are a work of art in progress'. By showing us the steps we ought to take in order to get better the book helps us to become the performers we've always dreamed to become."
—Ewa Jaślar, President of Polish Harp Society,
Harp teacher   Bielsko-Biala School of Music

"Drawing from a lifetime of world class performing experience, Dr. Carrol's passion and enthusiasm for self expression in all areas of life are truly inspiring. "Power Performance" is a valuable read for speakers, performers and anyone who is up for expanding their ability to express themselves."
—Bill Small, Singer/Songwriter, Performing Artist, Entrepreneur,
Life Coach

"I have known Carrol personally and professionally for many years. Her stunningly successful career path has led her to a lifetime of superior achievement; the most respected positions of authority; and national and international performances before the most coveted audiences. The secrets of her successes are finally revealed in her new book, *Power Performance.* Not only are her secrets important to performing artists, they can also be applied to the healing arts, helping others overcome life challenges while finding ways to acheive ones highest potential. Many will benefit by this great work!"
—Chuck Morris, Chairman and CEO, New Seasons Recovery Systems

DR CARROL'S

Power Performance

Dr. Carrol McLaughlin

 integrityink.us

www.integrityink.us
Tucson, Arizona
USA

Library of Congress Control Number: 2008938927

ISBN: 978-0-98186-330-6

Cover design: Karl Covington
Cover photograph: Robin Stancliff

Printed in the United States of America

To all those who have come before,
and all those who will follow,
Thank You! I Love You.
Special appreciation to Michael Colgrass,
Karen Kanak and my precious family.
                                    —Carrol McLaughlin

CONTENTS

Foreword

Carrol McLaughlin is an extraordinary harpist and a born performer. To her, performance has a broad meaning -- that life is a performance, on stage or off. Her intent in this book is to offer techniques culled from her vast experience throughout the world, as a musician, a teacher and a human being, to help those who wish to present themselves in every way at their very best. You will also learn skills that show how to develop rapport and communicate with others in teaching and personal relationships.

Her primary focus, quite naturally, deals with the pressures of appearing before people on public forums – playing a musical instrument, speaking to audiences or coaching corporate teamwork. She has created easy-to-learn exercises that will appeal to musicians, public speakers, trainers and managers, and that are designed to achieve quick, practical outcomes in high performance situations. This book will have special appeal to professionals but will benefit anyone who wishes to approach their work or their personal relationships with greater comfort and ease.

She has a deep belief in the potential of individuals, and that each person is his or her own best teacher. Being independent by nature, she wants others to develop their personal voice. She is more than a teacher or coach, she is an awakener, who shows you how you can develop yourself and enjoy taking ownership of the learning.

Although her exercises facilitate performance she is realistic and will tell you that no exercise will be of benefit without first preparing and rehearsing your material. She will ask you to drill your presentation 10 times before zero hour. She will tell you also that the exercises in this book must be repeated and practiced until they become habits in order to give full benefit. And she will show you how to pre-perform by imagining yourself using these skills at future events where they will be of special benefit.

This manual is a training method for those willing to take their performing development in their own hands by training themselves. I can endorse the value of these exercises having seen many of them in action. A number of them are especially effective done with a partner because you can enjoy both sharing the experience and benefiting from the feedback.

Those readers who are especially enterprising will make an effort to meet Carrol McLaughlin, an outstanding artist and an inspiring person. She is a living example of the principles she expouses and I highly recommend her and this book as models to both performers and teachers.

Michael Colgrass- Composer, Writer, Lecturer

–1–

LIFE PERFORMANCE

We Are All Performers

Every time you are in front of other people, presenting your opinion, your art, or your comments, you are performing. The success that you experience in your performance will have an effect on many other aspects of your life.

Whether it is making an important presentation for your company, speaking in front of the Parent Teacher Association, nailing a job interview or performing a solo piece on the stage of Carnegie Hall, you are the performer and your success rests upon how well you handle the stress and challenges of performing. Especially when it is important, the stress and pressure of presenting yourself at your best can be overwhelming and intimidating. The effect of wanting to do well can often cause you to do less than your best.

Performance Preparation

When you were in high school or university, and you knew there was a math test on Friday, you were sure to review the material the night before. When a lawyer prepares to take the Bar exam, there is an involved preparation course that each potential lawyer studies. Similarly, if someone is going to hike the Grand Canyon or run a ten- mile race, they know that getting in shape before the event is crucial.

As important as your upcoming job interview, speech to the PTA or solo recital might be to you, most of us do not prepare ourselves adequately for what we care so much about! In fact, we are often so concerned about the event (nervous if you will) that we do anything we can to *avoid* thinking about being in front of the public. I am often amazed that music majors at a university, who spend four hours per day for a year, learning and memorizing their music, will go on stage for the performance without knowing if they can walk in their new shoes or breathe in their concert gown or tuxedo!

The first time you do anything is usually the hardest. The first time you drove a car by yourself, it was a momentous occasion! Each approaching traffic light was a challenge, with you thinking to yourself, *"Oh-oh! What do I do now? Will it change color . . . oh dear it's yellow . . . should I stop? I'm going to race through. . . Whew! Oh, whoops! Now I am speeding . . . any cops around?"*

Then, after as little as a few dozen trips by yourself, you found you were able to carry on a conversation with a friend AND make a decision about a traffic light! It was "old hat," something that you felt confident about and were sure you could do with ease.

What would your upcoming business presentation feel like if it were the tenth or twentieth time you had given it? What if you *knew* you would ace it? What if you were so comfortable that the event became enjoyable? Imagine being able to love the experience and to look forward to it!

This book is dedicated to helping you not only perform at your optimum, but also to feel in harmony with yourself and the

2

information you are presenting, (whether that is musical notes or statistics). You will develop an unalterable personal belief in your capabilities and potential. You will approach challenges and opportunities in your life with more confidence, sure of your own excellence and convinced that you will do an outstanding job. You will learn sure-fire techniques which will ensure that every time you give a presentation it will be a fabulous Power Performance.

Preparation

Throughout this book, there will be exercises that will help you learn the material and allow the concepts to impact your life immediately. To start the first exercise, think of a challenging situation coming up in your life. It probably makes you feel a little queasy, just thinking about it. It may be speaking at a family reunion, making a difficult phone call, or giving a presentation at work. For musicians, it may be performing one piece in church or doing a full two-hour concert in a concert hall. If you have nothing pending that challenges your performing capabilities (very possible since the whole concept of *performing* may be too scary to contemplate), then I suggest you set something up, perhaps one month away. During the time leading up to the event you are concerned about, work through each chapter in this book and do the exercises at the end. You will be amazed how each tiny step makes you more confident and secure when under stress.

Be proud of yourself that you are committed to becoming a better speaker or musician or communicator. How admirable! For the sake of simplicity, this book will use "performer" and "performance" to refer to any time that you are presenting to others. You know when that is . . . the second the butterflies and self-doubt start going nuts, you are in performance mode. By

3

the end of your work on this subject, you will substitute butterflies with excitement, self-doubt with enthusiasm for what you are about to do.

Your Performing Environment

So that the tools of this book can have an immediate and personally rewarding impact, I want you to think about the performing situations or environments that are most stressful for you. There are hundreds of variations, from speaking up at company meetings to making telephone calls, to standing in front of a group of people and demonstrating a business concept, to memorizing a poem or a song, to preparing for a musical performance by memory.

Using the following worksheet, write out a typical situation which causes you to feel nervous and stressed. Try to imagine exactly how you feel, and be as honest with yourself as possible.

1. I am not comfortable when I am about to:

    _____

    _____

2. List your feelings when you think about doing this activity. For example, when you are about to address the public, do you feel butterflies in your stomach? Do your palms get sweaty? Do you hear a voice inside saying, "Why did I agree to do this? Is it over yet?" Describe your own personal experience when faced with "stage fright."

    _____

    _____

    _____

3. When you imagine giving this presentation or performance, where will you be physically? At home? In your business office? On a concert stage?

_____

_____

4. Describe what you will be doing, and where you will be **before** the performing activity starts. Will you be in your home? Will you be driving? Will this be unplanned, like receiving a daunting telephone call, over which you have no time control?

_____

_____

_____

5. How long will the activity (performance) actually take?

_____

_____

_____

By analyzing the surrounding environment, time, and situation of your most stressful performing times, you are already shining some light on the problem, making it less scary. Now that you have identified your stress inducing activity, know when, where and how it affects you, start taking a look at elements that you have control over.

Take Charge!

The first step is to take charge of any of the elements that you have control over. If it is a phone call that has you stressed, decide for yourself exactly when you want to make that call. Are you better able to deal with challenges in the morning or later in the day? Use the phone in your house or office that makes you feel more "in charge." Move some furniture around so that the area around the phone becomes more *you,* more empowering. Move some pictures next to the phone that remind you of family and friends that really believe in you. Try a candle beside the phone, and light it before difficult calls for moral support. Allow an answering machine to answer all your calls so that you have time to process and practice your response before returning the call, and return calls only when you are sure of your position.

Any other challenge has the same variables. If it is a concert, choose a date far enough in advance so that every piece of music can be memorized a minimum of one month before the concert. Investigate if special lighting might be used on the stage, making it more "you." Choose repertoire that truly expresses what you want to communicate to the audience, instead of playing what is "traditional" or "expected." Instead of being faulted for your unusual choices, you will be applauded for your creativity and individuality.

Think Sideways

Give yourself permission to think "outside the box." If it is a difficult business presentation that has you concerned, think about giving the presentation in a creative new way. Then instead of worrying about coming up to the standard of those who have presented before you, you can be the first and the best at showing the company a new approach. Think, "what if" or "why not." Brainstorm with some colleagues. What approaches might actually be *fun*? Make sure to allow yourself enough time to perfect the presentation, and follow the guidelines in this book to prepare the material thoroughly, and practice the presentation before the actual performance.

Let's look at some variables that you have control over when a stress-inducing situation occurs in real life.

Life's Mynopoly Board

Timing is crucial! Make sure that you have enough time to prepare thoroughly. There is really no such thing as being "over-prepared." To set up a time line in your mind, imagine the four sides of a game board. We'll call the board in your mind a "**my**nopoly" board.

Arrange the time between now and your presentation into four sections, each represented by one side of the board called stages one, two, three, and four. At the end of the game you collect a reward. On your board, every time you turn a corner the challenges and potential rewards in front of you change.

What might be the four pivotal points marking the stages? For example, if your challenging presentation is a job interview coming up in 16 days, that means each side of your own "mynopoly" board is four days long. The four cornerstones might be **stage 1)** arrange the day off, **stage 2)** plan wardrobe, **stage 3)** do practice run-throughs, **stage 4)** do job interview and collect reward for passing "GO!"

Further, think about *where* you want to give the performance, and what *content* you will present. To maximize the value of the information in this book, even if you don't have a required performing experience looming in your future, I urge you to set up a situation one or two months in the future, when you will be required to really perform. This will give you a goal to work towards and an immediate reward when you are able to perform more successfully and with less stress.

List below the performing experience that you have set up for yourself:

1. Today's Date:_____

2. Date of Performance:_____

3. Describe performance ... what type, etc.

   _____

4. Content of your performance. Is there any material you need to memorize? Do you need to write or research any material? If this is a concert, list your repertoire below.

   _____
   _____
   _____
   _____

5. My four cornerstones are:

   1) _____
   2) _____
   3) _____
   4) _____

Now you are ready to begin the process of becoming the master of your upcoming presentation. Remember to take one step at a time, processing each concept and incorporating it into your life and your habits. You are embarking on a magical voyage of self-discovery . . . how exciting!

Add one more important step – your reward. This should be a special treat for yourself, to celebrate your achievement. It needs to mean something to you, and feel special. Some people put money away to purchase an item they consider "luxurious." Other ideas: take a day off, get a massage, buy yourself some clothes, or take a trip. Fill in your reward .

When I complete my performance I will reward myself with:

_____

_____

Now, start imagining you are already celebrating your success, as if it has already happened. Bravo and congratulations! Luxuriate in how it will feel when you have successfully achieved your goal.

The journey to discovering your highest potential, and being able to share it with others, is one of the greatest *perks* life has to offer! The thrill of really being able to perform at a level you have dreamed about will instill you with a joy for life and deep self-satisfaction that will affect every part of your being.

Get ready for a marvelous journey of discovering that you really *can* do anything you dare to dream!

—2—

THE TOOLS OF SUCCESS

Open Your Toolbox

There is a wonderful definition of insanity . . . to keep doing the same thing over and over, expecting a different result. That is what many musicians and performers do. If they can't learn something or master playing a passage, they work *harder* at the passage, but usually in the same way! The new paradigm of practicing is to practice *smarter.* If you haven't learned something in a given amount of time, alter the way that you approach it. One of the reasons so many musicians and athletes suffer from overuse syndrome and tendonitis is that they push the body too far to learn something in a manner that has already proven it doesn't work. If the way you were practicing it already *worked,* you wouldn't need to practice it any more!

Far better than practicing *more* or *harder* is to understand what information you are trying to learn and approach it in different ways. For example, **see** the information or the notes, **hear** it, **feel** it, and experience it; envelope the material with all your senses. Then, much like putting information into a computer and carefully saving it in the right file for easy retrieval, practice retrieving the information enough times so you are *confident* that it will be there when you need it.
An important part of the secret is to become aware of *how* a human being learns and stores information. When applied to

11

your preparation for a Power Performance, these concepts have the potential to drastically alter (for the better!) your success on stage or in front of the public. As a performer who uses these principles on concert stages around the world, I know that this information is vital for anyone to have a more successful – and enjoyable – experience in any performing situation. In fact, I gave many recitals and concerts before ever learning that I could in fact practice *less time,* with *less chance of injury,* and *achieve more!* I used to live in fear of a "memory slip," where I would forget the next notes to play, or be speaking and totally forget the next sentence. What a horrible experience! Now I know that, because of my preparation, the distance between "staying on track" and playing at my best, or experiencing stage fright and having a bad experience on stage with memory slips, is light years apart . . . and the pathway I take is so deeply lined with "safety nets" that fear never comes into my consciousness.

My Journey

Having decided at the age of four to be a world-class harpist, I pursued this lofty goal by doing the "prescribed" things . . . getting a Master's from Juilliard, a Doctorate in music from the University of Arizona, studying in London with a famous (and cranky!) Russian harpist, playing debuts in Carnegie Hall and Wigmore, London, signing with Columbia Artists Management, etc. My path was one of hard work and perseverance . . . a boring paradigm but the best I knew at the time.

It was in 1984 that I first became aware that there were other options to working harder and longer. I was involved in a fascinating project in Los Angeles, working with the son of the late movie star Harpo Marx. Harpo was a member of the famous Marx Brothers who were internationally respected for their movies and comedy performances. I was learning and performing the music that Harpo had performed all over the world . . . and I had to play it note-for-note exactly the way Harpo played it, as part of my agreement with the Marx family. This was particularly tricky since Harpo had never learned how to read music; he learned everything by ear, and never developed an appreciation for what was really difficult on the harp! Therefore, all his pieces were unusually demanding.

Harpo's son, Bill, was transcribing Harpo's music for me and I had about 25 pieces to learn. Each piece was four to five pages long, and there was an important premiere of our concert coming up in a matter of weeks for all of Harpo's old friends and cronies from the motion picture industry. Throw into that mix Harpo's wife would be there and the pressure was immense!

At this time I was also Professor of Harp at the University of Arizona (and still am), and the University offered an Excellence in Performance workshop with Michael Colgrass, award-winning composer, author of "Lessons With Kumi, How I Learned To Perform With Confidence In Life And Work", Real People Press, and respected authority on Neuro Linguistic Programming (NLP). I attended the workshop and the information I learned was so incredible that it transformed my learning process and formed the basis for much of the information in this book.

Before this workshop, each *page* of the Harpo transcriptions had been taking me three to five hours to learn the notes, then another three to five hours to memorize. This was not looking good. With 25 arrangements, each at least four pages long, I was looking at a minimum of 800 hours of preparation . . . tough to fit into two weeks!

After learning the techniques presented at the workshop, which you will learn in this book, I was able to learn a whole page in two hours, and to memorize it accurately and solidly in two additional hours. My learning time was literally cut in half, and ten years later performing the same music on stage, *I still make fewer errors playing the music I learned in **half the time!***

Imagine yourself preparing for your next performance in *half your normal preparation time . . .* and anticipating a performance that is more thoroughly prepared and presented with more confidence than you have ever before experienced. Imagine being so sure of yourself that when you step up to a microphone you are relaxed and witty and enjoying yourself. Imagine how you will put your audience at ease, and establish an invaluable rapport with them - which will extend far beyond the limitations of your performance!

I am reminded of a television show my daughter used to watch when she was young entitled, "Herself the Elf." One elf would follow the others around as they crazily and ineffectively tried to fix things and say, "There must be an easier way to do this!" Well, that is true about your performing. There has to be an easier way to do this . . . and there *is*! It's called Power Performance.

The Magic of Power Performance

I call the set of tools that you will master in this book, Power Performance. Using these tools, you will be able to give a powerful, inspiring Power Performance in any arena. This will reap immeasurable rewards in terms of personal and professional success. Power Performance is defined as a strong, inspiring, confident performance in any area: speaking, negotiating, performing music – the list is endless and all encompassing. It ensures that the information you rehearse and practice is programmed into your mind and body in such a way that it can be easily and confidently pulled from your consciousness at any moment, and serve you without stress or self-doubt. This breakthrough strategy is a result of my twenty-year study of a mental tool called Neuro Linguistic Programming, or NLP, adapting these and other concepts of performing. The next chapters will discuss how aspects of Power Performance can jump-start your ability to perform without stress, in front of anyone, and allow you to overcome anything that is keeping you from experiencing the life you desire.

It is important to realize that every time you speak or participate in a conversation, you are performing. The success of that performance will be the outcome that you experience; what reaction you solicit from your audience. This is particularly important in a situation such as a doctor convincing a patient to stop smoking or alter their lifestyle to promote better health. Obviously the patient altering their behavior marks a successful performance on the part of the doctor. Other times the results can be less obvious, but important both to you and to the person you are speaking with. In teaching, negotiating, mediating, personal relationships, and a myriad of other situations the way that you communicate is a powerful tool and when viewed as a performance, can be honed to achieve the most beneficial results.

You have the power to impact how another person processes your words, and also how you feel about yourself following any conversation. As you build your Power Performance skills, you will learn to maximize your communication skills to achieve the results that you desire in every situation.

Where it All Started

A number of years ago, Dr. Milton Erickson, a famous psychiatrist from Phoenix, Arizona, was getting a great deal of attention in the psychiatric profession, even notoriety, because of his phenomenal success in treating phobia patients in a very short amount of time. He would cure insomnia, phobias, allergies, migrains, etc. in one session with the person. For example, a patient who was terrified to take the elevator up to an appointment would afterwards step comfortably into the elevator, "forgetting" that he or she had ever been afraid.

Two therapists from California, who co-founded NLP, Richard Bandler and John Grinder, set up video cameras, one aimed at the patient, and one focused on Dr. Erickson, to see what transpired in the therapy sessions. After close examination of the tapes, Bandler and Grinder observed that the secret of Erickson's success was his awareness that the mind stores and processes information, both factual and emotional, in different sensory categories or "sub-modalities."

Dr. Erickson had not invented anything . . . he simply had a genius for seeing patterns in the behavior of human beings. These realizations became one of the key models of the science of **Neuro Linguistic Programming**. Put simply:

Neuro: refers to the nerves. Anything we do or think is a result of a neurological impulse.

Linguistic: from the Latin, "Lingua" or language. This refers to the language or communication that gives the messages and commands to the nervous system, "putting the order in" for what action we want.

Programming: our ability to create behavior patterns that will achieve the specific outcome we desire.

Elements of NLP

Basic to Neuro Linguistic Programming is that every person has a number of ways of processing information. The three primary systems or *modes* of storing and retrieving information are **visual** (sight), **auditory** (hearing), and **kinesthetic** (touch or feeling). Other perception systems include olfaction and gustation, being the senses of smell and taste, respectively. Although olfaction and gustation are very important, they have little influence upon the learning processes important in performance. We will be concentrating on the three "key players": visual, auditory, and kinesthetic.

Often you can tell what mode someone is using by the words they use. Try listening carefully to a number of different people's conversations. Pay careful attention to the words they choose.

You will discover that some people tend to think of their world in **visual** terms. Without listening too long you probably would hear phrases such as:

"*Looks* like a great plan."
"I can *see* what you mean."
"What a *bright* idea!"

Some people favor processing information from an **auditory** point of view. A person thinking in an auditory mode might say:

"I *hear* what you're saying."
"*Sounds* good to me."
"It didn't *ring true*."

A person who is operating from a **kinesthetic** or feeling mode might be overheard using phrases such as:

"I *feel like* we're going to have trouble."
"That's a *heavy* subject."
"I have an *overwhelming* urge."

While you are tuned in (an **auditory** image, right?) to listening to modalities people are using, there are some additional things to try that are illuminating and very worthwhile. Consider the concept of **rapport**. The dictionary describes rapport as "a relationship, especially one of mutual trust or affinity." Mutual trust or affinity usually comes from feeling a bond or similarity with someone. It can be said that all effective communication takes place within the framework of rapport. Try this experiment to establish immediate rapport with someone you just met.

First, listen carefully to what words they are using. Then, *respond in the same modality* to establish rapport. Your conversation might sound like this:

Person A: "Looks like you get the idea."
Person B: "I can really see what you mean."
Person A: "Let me clarify this one concept for you."
Person B: "You have brightened my whole day!"

Unfortunately, the opposite is also possible. Without trying, we can put ourselves *out of rapport* simply by using words that the other person cannot relate to. Imagine this scene in a lounge. A married couple is talking.

Man: "I don't *see* what your problem is."
Woman: "I *feel* like you don't understand what I am saying."
Man: "*Show* me what I have done wrong."
Woman: "I don't get the *sense* that you understand."
Man: "*Looks* like we just can't agree."
Woman: "Don't you *feel* how we are slipping apart?"

18

Obviously, the man is in **visual** and the woman in **kinesthetic**. If one person in the above discussion had realized that they were talking "different languages," then that person would have been able to bridge the communication gap and start to say words that made the other feel more in rapport. For example,

Man: "I don't *see* what your problem is."
Woman: "Let me *show you* what I mean. It is not clear to me that you are concerned about my feelings."
Man: "Oh! Why didn't you say that before? I *see* it now."

Create Harmony!

The second that you start to "speak the same language" as the people you are talking with, you have established rapport with them. Being in rapport has very long-reaching ramifications. As teachers, it is imperative to be aware of what mode your students are functioning in, so that you can communicate with them in a way that they can easily access. This is particularly important if the student is having difficulties or is feeling overwhelmed, because they are less able to "bridge the gap" to understand other modalities when their own sensations are in stress. As family members, it is important to listen closely when your family speaks to you. Are you in rapport? Are you really listening to not only what they are saying, but also *how they are saying it?* Are you willing to take the extra moment to answer in a manner that they will feel comfortable with? Imagine the ramifications of having a truly harmonious, team-building conversation with your spouse or child. I cannot imagine a more important stage for a Power Performance!

Look Around (and Listen, Feel...)

Another eye-opening exercise is to watch people on television, particularly politicians. Very often a good speaker will make sure to include all three modes in every important statement. For example, they might say, "I can *see* clearly that we must *join* together in a strong, united and proud group, *singing* the praises of our country in a *clear, thunderous, overwhelming* voice. This makes no real sense (oh well, I was *trying* to be a politician), but it does have impact for people accessing all three modalities.

Try it Out

To strengthen your own potential it is important to be aware of visual, auditory and kinesthetic images and references. Do this exercise with a friend: say a two-part sentence, which alternates modalities in the middle. For example:

"I can *see* that we are going to have to *feel* this out carefully." So this started in *visual* (see) and went to *kinesthetic* (feel).

Have the second person respond with a two-part sentence, *beginning in the modality you used last and then adding another different modality:* so, they would start in *kinesthetic* and end in another mode of their choice:

"It is a *heavy* subject (kinesthetic) but I bet we can throw some *light* (visual) on it." A response to that might be, "I can just *see* (visual) them *singing* (auditory) our praises."

As you proceed with your day, keep your attention on how people around you are communicating. Stretch yourself to use modes that are not your norm. If you typically would say, "*looks* good to me" (visual) try saying, "*feels* like a great plan" (kinesthetic). See how far you can go with this, and you will be amazed at what images you will come up with. Gustatory or olfactory words might also be included, with phrases such as, "Smells fishy to me," or "What a scrumptious idea."

When Something Doesn't Quite Fit In the Groove

Sometimes you will find a word that does not fit into the representational system categories we have been exploring. It might be that the word is ambiguous and means two different things, such as the word *light,* which could be interpreted as *visual* (I see the light) or *kinesthetic* (a light-weight idea). There may also be words that do not refer to a specific sensory system. Examples of this would be words such as *wonder, seems, think.* Ambiguous or non-referring words will be interpreted by the listener in their own choice of mode.

You are now well on your way to listening differently, and having the power to realize how others are thinking, and to interact more effectively with them. Following are some suggestions to integrate this knowledge completely, and help you become more successful at communication. This will impact many aspects of your life because you are learning to communicate, and to think, in exciting new ways.

MAKIN' IT HAPPEN ... choose
3 of these ideas and put them into practice TODAY!

1. Engage in a conversation with a friend and listen to determine if they use more **visual, auditory,** or **kinesthetic** words and images.

2. Listen in to other people's conversations. Notice if the people are in rapport or not. See how often you can identify words taken

from one of the representational systems of visual, auditory or kinesthetic.

3. Ask a friend or family member to pay close attention when you talk to them to see if you favor one of the representational systems. Have them bring this to your attention . . . and then see for yourself if that's what you always tend to do: feel out if that is how you like to think; or decide if it "sounds like you."

4. The next occasion that you have to work with a younger child or student, be very attentive to the word choices they make, then respond in a similar way. If they are using visual terms, try to include many visual examples in what you are presenting. Similarly, a child using auditory based words will relate best by being read to or by listening to the way a phrase should be played on an instrument. If the student is indicating a kinesthetic preference, have them play a passage or actually try something out so they can *feel*/how it goes.

5. Talk to a friend, coach or fellow performer about a recent performance you have given. Have them write down all the images you used as you speak about your performance, particularly visual, kinesthetic or auditory based. It will be enlightening to you to realize that you think of your own performance success either in terms of how it looks sounds or feels. Now try to go back over your recollection of the performance and "fill in the blanks." If you said, "The Mozart was bright and radiant," (obviously a visual image), try to make that image three dimensional for yourself by thinking about how it felt to play (kinesthetic), and how rich the harmonies were (auditory). You will still have the same strong reaction, but you are allowing yourself to "use more colors of the palette" to paint for yourself the picture of your art.

6. For one day, try to think about your own preferences in terms of storing and retrieving information in kinesthetic, auditory or

visual mode. Usually there is one mode that is favored. If you have done exercise number 3 above, you may have already realized that you tend to favor one mode over the others. *Now, for the real fun!* For one day, try to force yourself to think and talk in a mode other than the one you are most comfortable in. If it is your habit to say, "I see what you mean," say and think, "I feel the impact of what you are saying," or "I hear you."

By using different modes than we are used to for thinking, processing and speaking, we enlarge our potential for creativity and increase our problem-solving abilities. By assisting our children and students to utilize all three modes, we are giving them an extraordinary gift . . . increasing their potential for excellence in anything they choose!

—3—

THE EYES HAVE IT!

The Visual Mode

As you are reading this, recall exactly what is on the top shelf of your refrigerator. Imagine that someone is going to give you $10.00 if you can name every item correctly. *See* the fridge with the door open and name every item . . . preferably remembering their exact position. (Extra imaginary money will be awarded if you can remember how full the milk carton is or how much jam or margarine is in the container, etc.)

What did you do while you were concentrating very hard and trying to recall a visual image of the fridge? Most probably, you glanced up towards the ceiling, probably towards your left. Perhaps your eyes moved from left to right, or in some instances they defocused and stared straight ahead. These eye movements were a natural strategy of your brain to assist you to remember an image of your fridge, so you could decipher what you wanted to remember.

One of the most fascinating and important elements of Neuro Linguistic Programming that came out of the tapes made of Milton Erickson, is the fact that **where your eyes move to** has a direct relationship with **what mode you are accessing; in effect, your eye positions show how you are thinking.**

To access visual information, your eyes will most often look up. You are actually looking up and seeing an image of the fridge inside your mind. Then you can "look around" and see the answers to what you want to know. When outstanding spellers are taught to spell, they learn to *see the word* in the air, up and to their left. In fact, it is even more successful to imagine writing the word in the air. When the person is then asked to spell the word, they look up and to the left and simply read the correct spelling from the word they see in front of them.

There are many useful applications of this. If you want to remember a telephone number, imagine writing it up in the air. Practice looking back at it four or five times, maybe even change the color of ink you wrote it in (in your imagination). When you want to retrieve the telephone number, look up and see it. It's almost like cheating – just read the numbers you see in your mind's eye.

This could also be invaluable when you meet new people and you want to remember their names. Not only could you install a picture of the person's name up in your **visual recall** (up and to the left) but you could put a picture of the person up there too. If the person was wearing a red sweater you might see their name emblazoned on a red sweater in your mind. If you had to remember that the person designed aircraft missiles, the picture you put in your mind of that person might be a man riding astride a missile with his name painted on the side of the missile. This image would be particularly helpful to you if the man tended to intimidate you. By painting a very human and slightly humorous picture of him in your own mind, you have robbed him of the power of intimidation over you, because you don't "see him in that light."

Let's try another example. Think of a friend or colleague who you saw within the last two days. Recall what clothes they were wearing when you last saw them. What colors? How did their face look? Were they carrying something? Now, imagine that same person but *they just got a punk haircut and colored the right half of their head bright pink*!

When you recalled the visual image of your friend, your eyes most likely looked *up and to the left*. This is called **visual recall.** (For some people visual recall can also be looking straight ahead with the eyes slightly defocused but the effect is the same). When you saw the same person but altered the image, (instant punk), you were accessing an area called **visual construct** because you are taking an image you already have, and altering or constructing that image. To access that visually constructed image, your eyes look *up and to your right*. A simple way to think of this is that to your left is the past, the way things have been, and to the right is how you could construct them in the future

The Auditory Mode

Imagine yourself playing a piece at your last practice session, or hear your voice explaining something to another person at a meeting or speaking engagement. You might choose an important conversation with your boss or a work colleague. Hear the timbre and sound of your voice. Remember exactly how it sounded.

As you access this memory, your eyes will probably go *horizontally towards your left ear*, parallel with your ears. This is **auditory recall.** Now, think of the same event but alter it slightly. For example, imagine that your practice session had a full orchestra behind you, or you heard the most fantastic tone imaginable from your instrument . . . or your voice was magically amplified to be louder and more authoritative than ever before. Your eye movement, as you altered the auditory track in your memory, will be *horizontal and to your right*. This is **auditory construct.** Similar to **visual recall** and **visual construct, auditory recall** will always be to your left and **auditory construct** (an altered image in the future) will be to your right.

If you tried the preceding exercise and instead of your remembered image being on your left, it was on your right, there is a chance that you have the two areas of information mirrored in your mind. This is not a problem, only an indication that your **recall** (history) and **construct** (future) access areas are mirrored to be on the opposite side of what is most common. If you are finding that everything I ask you to access on your *left* feels more appropriate to access on your *right,* then simply make that alteration for yourself as you are reading. That is, if I refer to *up and to your left*, you might be more comfortable with *up and to your right.* Sometimes this is true for people who are naturally left-handed – but try it out and see what fits! For most people, however, **visual remembrance or recall** will be accessed by looking up and to their left.

Here is another auditory exercise. Remember when you last heard a live performance of a Symphony orchestra, and recall the sound of the concert. Now, imagine what that same music would sound like, played by an out-of-tune bagpipe orchestra. (Rolling your eyes in disgust is not an NLP – acknowledged process!) The music of the symphony was most likely accessed by looking to your left at eye level (auditory recall.) When the sound was altered to bagpipes (auditory construct) your eyes probably moved straight across and to your right.

Now that you are aware of where your mind accesses information naturally, it is possible to learn to store information consciously in those modes, and also to use the eyes to help you remember. For example, if you came out of a large shopping mall and could remember where you parked your car, you might look up and to the left and try to see an image of pulling into the parking spot, noticing which way you were pointed, what other kinds of cars were around you, and seeing which direction you walked when you got out of the car. It is even more effective if you consciously implant the visual image of where your car is parked, before leaving your car.

The Kinesthetic Mode

Imagine that you are stroking an animal that you are fond of . . . maybe a family pet. Feel in your mind the sensation of the fur against your hand, and the warmth of the animal snuggling up against you. As you recall this **kinesthetic** (or *feeling)* sensation, your eyes most probably looked downward and to your right.

In contrast to visual and auditory, kinesthetic does not have past and future or remembrance and construct parts. All kinesthetic thoughts are accessed in the same area, which is down and to your right. Kinesthetic refers both to how something actually *feels*, like the soft fur of a kitten, or how it *feels* emotionally, such as fearful, nervous, excited or content.

Obviously, kinesthetic will impact you very strongly since it has a direct connection to your emotions. This also means kinesthetic is where your nervousness and fear of performance exists. Further, when you have an adrenaline rush from the human fight or flight response, that experience is processed completely in your kinesthetic.

Unfortunately, this often happens when we are asked to speak or perform in front of others.

As you progress further honing your Power Performance tools you will learn to control the power your kinesthetic tendencies have in times of stress. When performing, relying on auditory, and especially visual modes, is a much safer option. Realizing you are in control of how you process is an important step in overcoming stress in all aspects of your life.

Internal Dialogue

If you look down and to your *left,* you are accessing an area that is very important to a performer, that of **internal dialogue.** This is the little voice inside you that speaks to you in your mind. It is often what we hear when we "think of something." Sometimes it is the voice that reminds us to do something such as, "Remember to pick up milk on the way home." Sometimes internal dialogue can take the form of a disapproving voice that is telling us we didn't do something right, that we are not good enough, or that we are about to make a mistake. Unfortunately, most of us have experienced such negative self-talk as, "I am so stupid," or, "Here comes that hard passage I always screw up," or, "I can never remember names." As a performer it is extremely important to become aware of this part of your thought process, and learn how to use this knowledge to your benefit. In a future chapter you will learn how to use your internal dialogue to be your coach, friend and assistant.

Here's Lookin' at You

Following will see a diagram that summarizes where the eyes move to access different information. ***This is you looking out***, not you looking at someone! For clarification, hold this book up against your chest with the picture facing out and establish firmly in your mind which is your right and left as you look at this diagram.

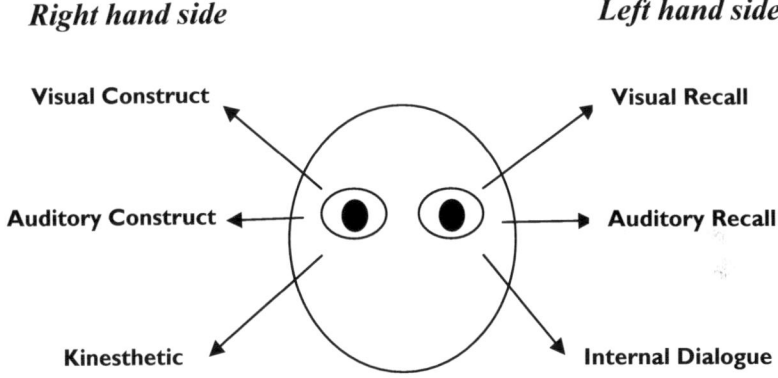

The Team Approach

Often the mind will want to access a combination or conglomeration of information which has been stored in visual, auditory, kinesthetic and internal dialogue. Likewise, it may want to switch back and forth between a remembered idea and a new (constructed) strategy. This involves the eyes moving back and forth between the modes as different ideas are accessed.

Here is an example: Imagine that the phone rings and it is someone very important to you. They ask you a career-altering question. Maybe it is a major concert tour which happens to come at your busiest time. Maybe it is your boss asking if you would move your family to Alaska to accept a new position. Before answering this important question, you will probably run your answer by in your mind. You are *hearing your response* internally before you say it out loud (internal dialogue). As you do this exercise you may find your eyes switching back and forth from down and to your left (internal dialogue) to down and to your right (kinesthetic). This is a perfectly understandable and predictable reaction. Your mind has come up with a possible answer, but wants to switch to kinesthetic mode to experience how the answer feels.

Eye movements are wired to the senses. By watching a person's eyes you can determine which mode they are using; if they are seeing, hearing or feeling. If you were to ask someone a question and then watch his or her eye movements, you might see something like this:

Person A: I would like to offer you a wonderful job. It will be a great career opportunity, but it involves moving to Inuvik. Can you see yourself living in the Arctic?

Person B might start with his eyes up and to the left, picturing Inuvik.

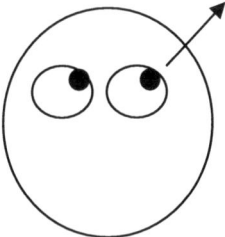

Note: this is the person looking **at you**

His eyes then might move up and to the right, picturing himself and his family living and working in the Arctic in the future. (This is Visual Construct.)

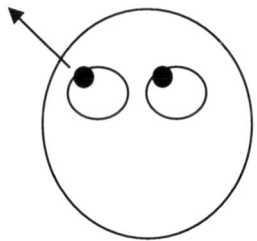

Next, his eyes might go down and to the right, thinking how much he dislikes feeling cold. (He is accessing Kinesthetic.)

Then, his eyes might look down and to the left, imagining telling his wife that the family was moving to the Arctic. (Internal Dialogue)

One more check down and to the right, seeing how it feels to have that discussion with his spouse . . . and how it will feel to even broach the subject! Whew! Overwhelming.

Next the eyes go to the right parallel to the ears, hearing what reaction he might get from Person A if he tried for a delay tactic.

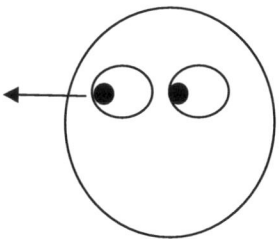

And he responds to Person A, "Gee, I don't know what to say. Can I have a few days to think about it?"

It is important to remember that all of these eye movements are strategies that are inherent to all human beings. Our eyes do this *naturally* and without conscious awareness. Every person has the capabilities to use all the modes, though often one becomes more habitual than others. By becoming aware of how your mind is processing through noticing these eye movements, as well as being able to read how others are processing, allows you the potential to literally alter the way you think and impact others.

You Are in Control

Imagine this scene: A young boy is playing baseball with his friends in a driveway. He throws the ball and instead of it going where he intended, the ball flies straight towards his parents' large front room window . . . and disaster! The ball goes through the window, shattering glass everywhere. His father opens the front door and yells at his son, livid with anger. The boy reluctantly goes inside, eyes downcast, feeling horrible and terrified of what his father will do (he is in kinesthetic.)

The man yells at his son, saying that this is unacceptable and that he has *told* his son not to play ball in front of the window. At first the boy continues to look down at the ground. He feels ashamed and sorry. He didn't mean to do it. He feels like the earth is opening up and he is descending into a deep pit of despair. His eyes fill with tears.

The father keeps yelling about responsibility and respect and how the boy has let him down. The boy has heard this before and by now is getting kind of tired of this verbal barrage. His eyes veer down and to his left. He hears his own voice saying, "Okay, Okay, I get the point! I will pay for the window. Nobody died, for heaven's sake! Give it a break!" (Internal dialogue)

Unaware that he has lost his audience, the man is working himself up more and more. Obviously the boy doesn't *get it* and the father is going to make sure the boy understands that behavior like this cannot be tolerated. The boy finally looks up (into visual). He sees that tomorrow they are going to play ball at Tommy's house. He sees that he left his baseball glove lying on the driveway. He hopes his mother won't run over it when she drives in, (he plays the scene in his head, looking up and to the right, and realizes that his mother's car will stop a few feet before hitting the glove. Whew!) Now he sees himself and his friends playing a little league game at that great park where he once hit a home run. At this point, anything the father says falls on deaf ears. No matter what is said, it will not cause the boy to feel remorse because the boy is **not accessing his kinesthetic** *or feelings.* The boy is happily visualizing his next home run in a ballpark far away.

Perhaps we can all learn something from the boy's natural reaction. I have found myself in many sad movies, staring at the ceiling so that I will not start crying. (If you don't access your kinesthetic, you don't react in an emotional manner.) As musicians and public speakers, we often must perform at very emotional occasions, such as a funeral. It is inappropriate to allow your kinesthetic to become involved and to get "choked up" or emotional. How perfect that you carry with you the most successful tool for maintaining your equilibrium! By looking up at the ceiling and accessing **visual**, you can "short circuit" your emotions from running wild, and maintain an *image* of professionalism. Similarly, if a colleague or boss is hauling you across the carpet (what a kinesthetic image!) for a perceived error you made, you have two options. You can either "dive in" to your kinesthetic and feel rotten, or glance quickly upwards and be able to *see it* in perspective. In fact, helping your boss to throw some light on the problem, or perhaps to *see* your point of view might be very worthwhile.

Maximizing the use of each of the modes of visual, auditory and kinesthetic is invaluable as you work towards reaching your highest potential. See, hear, and feel the impact of mastering this integral part of Power Performance. The following chapter will examine more specific ways to use these tools to achieve greater Power Performance success.

MAKIN' IT HAPPEN ... choose
3 of these ideas and put them into practice TODAY!

1. Below is a list of questions. Sit opposite another person and ask them these questions (or similar ones you think of yourself). Watch carefully where their eyes go. After ten or 15 minutes, have them ask you questions and watch where your eyes go to access the information needed to answer. After doing the exercise, discuss what you each noticed. Can you

make any observations about the other person's eye movements? Could you see their eyes accessing differently for visual, auditory or kinesthetically based information? Did they tend to access one mode more than the others?

- ❖ Describe the outside entrance to your home.
- ❖ Which side of Lincoln's face is on a penny? Which direction is he facing?
- ❖ Visualize a pink triangle above a blue rectangle.
- ❖ Of all the members of your family, whose voice do you like the most?
- ❖ Which instrument is loudest, the piano or the harpsichord?
- ❖ When was your last performance or business presentation? How did it go?
- ❖ Make a picture in your mind of a large, fat toad.
- ❖ Now make a picture in your mind of a large fat fuchsia toad.
- ❖ Imagine your favorite animal. Imagine petting him. What does he/she like the most?
- ❖ Remember the feeling of jumping into a cold pool. Now imagine yourself in a wonderfully hot Jacuzzi. Now jump back and forth between the two in your mind.
- ❖ Hear in your head the sound of an ambulance or police car. Hear how the sound changes as the ambulance goes past you.

2. Decide that today you are going to be extremely aware of the words that people use in conversation. You will notice that body posture also echoes what mode a person is accessing. Visual will tend to be very erect, with shoulders back and head held high (imagine a statue of Napoleon envisioning success in battle, or the Statue of Liberty). Kinesthetic will be with the head tilted, looking down, sometimes with the chest sagging in and shoulders rounded. (Imagine Rodin's statue of *"The*

Thinker".) Breathing also will alter. Visual accessing will tend to be a shallow, high breath whereas a kinesthetic accessing will cause the person to breath deeply and slowly. Also notice if the person is using gestures (kinesthetic) as a part of their conversation.

3. The next time you are working with a student or someone who has asked you for help, ask them to describe the problem. See if they answer in terms of visual, auditory or kinesthetic. Try to respond to them in the mode they are accessing.

4. By listening to yourself in conversation and also noticing your eye movements, decipher for yourself which of the modes you habitually favor. Notice what kinds of words you use, and if it is more comfortable for you to tell a story to someone, to paint them a visual picture of what you would like, or to try to get them to feel your point of view. It is particularly helpful if you use the "buddy system," asking another person to help you by bringing to your attention when you use a sensory-specific image or word.

5. Decipher what mode your "significant other" or family member favors. One of my husband's favorite phrases is, "Sounds good to me." By realizing that he therefore processes often in auditory mode, I find that conversations are particularly successful with him when I begin with, "Can I talk this through with you and see how it sounds?" We are immediately in rapport.

6. Watch an actor or spokesperson on television, and notice where their eyes move as they speak, and what types of words they choose. Obviously, it will not help to watch the news anchorperson who is reading the cue cards . . . but it is very telling to watch a politician as he is giving a speech, or a person who is being interviewed.

–4–

YOUR LEADING MODE

What Makes You Tick?

Many people have a favorite lead **sense** or **leading mode**, one sensory system that they favor above the others, and tend to use most frequently. In my particular case, I have always been an extremely **kinesthetic** person. I like to *sense* what to do, and *feel* my way through situations. Recently, I watched myself on a television interview that was made a number of years ago. For every question the interviewer asked me, I accessed my answer by looking down and to my right, into kinesthetic . . . even to answer the question, what was my own name!

In fact, I have spent most of my life so kinesthetically-based that the other two modes, those of auditory and visual, have been under-used and under-developed. As I have given lectures and workshops on NLP throughout the United States and other countries, I have found that many people also have one or two modes of storing information that have never been used enough to develop fully. The wonderful thing is that once this is brought to our attention, it is very fast and easy to get the under-developed mode or modes up and running . . . so much so that the new strategies can become your strongest choices for storing and retrieving information. I now count heavily on my power of visual recall to remember important information. I make it a point to imbed that information consciously and firmly into my visual memory. (For example, I will look up and to the left and **see** the information, or see myself remembering to do something.)

In the first chapter I mentioned that I took a workshop with Michael Colgrass (whom I consider the *Merlin* of NLP), which opened my eyes to Neuro Linguistic Programming. During this course, Michael realized that I was dealing primarily in the kinesthetic mode. He asked me to stand in front of the class for half an hour and perform an experiment. All I had to do was to *look up!* I obligingly raised my eyes and started staring at the ceiling. As I did so, my whole physiology changed. My complexion gained color and my breathing moved to a higher position in my chest. I found myself straightening my shoulders and I raised my chin to stand taller. People watching this transformation said to me after the class that it was truly amazing how much my face and complexion changed as I realized or "saw" a different reality for myself than I had ever previously experienced.

This simple exercise, of staring *upwards* had an amazing and far-reaching effect on me. It was as if I had traveled down a corridor hundreds of times and thought I knew what was there, but suddenly someone opened a door along the hallway and the corridor was flooded with sunshine and *energy!*
I was suddenly made aware of the world of visual images . . . simply by making myself access my visual mode. Michael gave me a follow-up assignment, to look up for five minutes per day until it felt comfortable. (In the class, looking up and accessing visual for the first time had been quite uncomfortable–very foreign and a little unnerving. After practicing it several times, it became natural and easier.) Now visual accessing is one of my strongest mental tools.

The result of this change in how I accessed things (literally, changing my view of the world), had many repercussions . . . all positive. I started storing things in my visual memory that I wanted to remember, and was amazed at how easy it was. (Trying to remember everything in kinesthetic meant I had *feelings* associated with every thought, which can be exhausting! For example, "Remember to pay the phone bill" would bring with it feelings of guilt and internal dialogue about how late it was, that I was terrible with keeping my checkbook up to date, and that I always put things off and I was a rotten person . . . and on and on! How much easier to just see myself paying the bill.)

Try This for Yourself

Do you have an activity that really bogs you down? Maybe it is answering mail, or sending out letters. Maybe it is doing income tax. The list of possibilities is endless. One common problem for many people is returning telephone calls.

If you really have difficulty facing this activity, there is a high probability that you are thinking about that activity in kinesthetic terms. For example, if the problem is returning phone calls, here is how your thought process might go:

1. *I have to call George.*
2. *I am so late in returning his call!*
3. *I feel rotten that I have not called him yet.*
4. *I am not sure what I want to tell him. What if he is mad that I have not called him before now?*

Finally the guilt and emotions of the phone call overwhelm you, and you put the phone call off yet once again. Kinesthetic won.

Now, contrast that with the following scenario:

43

1. *I need to call George.*
2. *I see the piece of paper with his number.*
3. *I can see myself calling him quickly and chatting for a few minutes.*
4. *There is the phone and there is the number. After I call him my day will seem clearer and brighter.*
5. *CALL!*

What made all the difference was that when you thought about the call in visual mode, it stopped having all the emotional attachment. It became business, not personal. Instead of it being an overwhelming, guilt-ridden chore, it became what it actually is; a five minute job that you could *see* yourself doing.

Performing in Visual

Perhaps the most important change for me when I "opened up the channel" to use my visual powers occurred in performance. Previously, if I was giving a speech, I would have the information I was going to say stored in my kinesthetic memory. I would remember how I felt about the content and the emotions behind my words. I even stored people's names in my kinesthetic memory, along with how I felt about them, if I liked them or not, if they made me feel comfortable, etc. Then when I got nervous or self-conscious about making an introduction, (already kinesthetic,) I would be overwhelmed with self-doubt and not be able to access their names – even the names of friends that I had known for years. The storing of this information in my Kinesthetic did not allow me to access the information when I was under pressure and feeling stressed to perform well.

Similarly, I had learned all of my music for concerts in kinesthetic. This presented quite a problem. In a performance situation, I would often feel a surge of adrenaline, as most of us do. Since adrenaline affects how we feel, and all my knowledge was stored in kinesthetic, experiencing the adrenaline coming on was like a tidal wave engulfing me. It would obliterate any trace of what I was supposed to remember, and I would be left with a "memory slip" or "blackout."

Sometimes this would happen backstage, sometimes as I looked at the audience, or sometimes within the performance itself, particularly if I felt unprepared or was concerned about one portion of the piece. I was still performing successfully, mostly because I worked so diligently on my preparation that I could fill in if something went wrong. But looking back now, what a lot of unnecessary energy I expended on stage, just worrying that I would forget something!

The essence of Power Performance is learning that there are different ways to retrieve information, and tried-and-true processes that you can use to ensure mental clarity on stage. This knowledge has made performing and communicating easier and more joyful. Now I can communicate the beauty of the music, not my own anxiety about my performance! My belief that I will **not** forget my music or my speech has boosted my level of performance to a much higher level than I would have ever attained without the knowledge of these powerful tools.

Triple Channel Learning

Imagine this scene. You are driving to the airport to catch a flight. You have very little time to accomplish this . . . in fact, there is just barely enough time to make the flight! As you turn out onto the main thoroughfare, you see a huge traffic jam. Quickly, you assess the situation and realize that this route is not going to work. You exit to another road, not the tried-and-true path you are used to taking, but certainly a route that works! You arrive at your destination with time to spare, make your flight, and congratulate yourself on your ingenuity.

Imagine the frustration you would feel if you didn't have an alternate route and if you had missed your flight. This outcome is unacceptable so most of us, consciously or unconsciously, usually have an alternate plan somewhere in our minds. Counting on only one route is simply too risky.

And yet, as musicians and speakers, often we take the huge chance that our one mental pathway of information will not have a traffic jam! Storing all of our learned information in one mode, means we are counting 100% that we will be able to access that information when we need it; in our example above, that the one road to the airport will be open. This is very dangerous, especially if the mode you have chosen to store your knowledge in is kinesthetic. It is far better to store your knowledge in all three modes of *visual, auditory* and *kinesthetic.* This way, if one flow of information is interrupted, your mind will simply shift to another mode, like having a secondary road in a traffic jam. You will be able to   continue on as if nothing happened.

To learn in all three modes is called **Triple Channel Learning**. Triple Channel learning, as created by Michael Colgrass, involves the storing of information in all three senses so that if one of them "goes out" you have a back up. In case any one of the senses fails there are two other ways to remember. It means that for every sentence you need to speak or every phrase you want to play, you have mastered how it *looks,* how it *sounds,* and how it *feels.*

Strengthening Your Tools

The Visual Mode

A few years ago, my husband took a very expensive review course for passing the exam to become a Certified Public Accountant. On the last day of the course the teacher instructed everyone on one of the most important things they could do to ensure a good grade. The students were to hold their book up to their left and visually scan each page before going into the exam.

The teacher was accomplishing two things: first, the mind received a reconfirmation of the visual information it had learned. Second, the teacher was having each student put themselves into visual mode right before entering the exam room. This short-circuited any nervousness or feelings of inadequacy that the students might feel at that time, because they were now accessing their visual mode, *not* kinesthetic! Looking up not only accesses your stored visual memories, but causes you to process any new experience in visual terms.

Look Up!

Accessing visual mode can be one of our greatest tools for fighting stage fright or nervousness Every time you need to perform in front of anyone, take a deep breath (this is a "separator" allowing you to experience something new,) and *force your eyes up to survey the ceiling* for at least three minutes before making your entrance. Envision or visualize in your mind walking out in front of the audience, and carrying with you an aura of self-confidence and brilliant energy. See yourself beginning to talk or play your instrument, relaxed and self-assured, recalling one of your best past performances.

Another important tool is to have a copy of your music or your speech backstage and, much like the CPA students, hold the music or words up and to your left. Visually scan each page. Now, maintain this "visual head space" as you approach your performance. It is very important to maintain your concentration after these exercises. Keep the eyes up and your shoulders back and confident. Minimize interaction with others so that you may maintain your ideal performance state. As you walk onto the stage, *stay in visual mode!* If you allow your eyes to become glued to the floor, and your shoulders to slump, you are not only courting disaster by accessing your feelings (kinesthetic), and your internal dialogue,(auditory), but you are communicating to your audience (and to yourself!) that you don't feel very confident about what you are about to do.

Check out the Ceiling

I cannot count the number of backstage ceilings I have studied in my career! I was recently the featured soloist, performing with a major Japanese orchestra in front of a sold out audience of 7,000 people. It was an opening night performance of a concerto I had recently learned. The stress was enormous! I knew I would have to use all the tools I had to overcome my own inhibitions and perform at my best. I arrived at the hall with time to spare and visualized in my mind every aspect of the performance, from walking on the stage through to my bow. For ten minutes before I needed to go on stage, I stood quietly backstage, apart from the other performers *staring up.*

That evening I had the most crystal-clear focus imaginable on stage. I only recall one extraneous thought, which occurred after the second movement of the three-movement piece when I heard my interior dialogue say, "Oh my gosh . . . this is going *perfectly!*" Instantly realizing the potential danger in switching out of visual mode to engage in internal dialogue, I quickly pictured in my mind the opening page of music for the third movement and became totally involved in the performance again.

I toured Japan as soloist with that orchestra, and I had an interesting experience with the conductor. He was very highly respected throughout Japan, but he was feared by the musicians in the orchestra because his tempos were so erratic. Sometimes he would conduct a piece very slowly, then another time it would be so fast it was impossible to play. By the first rehearsal I realized that he was extremely emotional, and was conducting from a purely kinesthetic mode of reference. If he felt enthused by the performance, his tempos would speed up . . . very dangerous when tackling a difficult performance. Somber and melancholy portions of the piece could drag on forever, as his tempos got slower and slower. Obviously, it was in my own best interest to have the tempos at an idea speed for my performance. I devised the following strategy. In order to have him maintain perspective and not be a victim of his own over-active kinesthetic mode, backstage right before the performance, I asked him how the audience looked and if he could see us nailing the performance, or similar visually-leading questions. The result was fantastic – he conducted comfortably and at reasonable tempos and the whole experience was a wonderful success.

Building Your Visual Strength

In the weeks leading up to your speech or public performance, here are some ways that you can ensure that you are getting a strong visual picture of what you want to learn! Make a habit of including these ideas into your preparation.

❖ If you are learning music, raise your music stand above the level of your head and slightly to your left so that your eyes are in *visual recall* as you are learning the music.

❖ If you are reading a speech or material that you need to memorize, hold the book or script up and to your left.

❖ Away from your instrument, practice recalling the number of the page and which line every phrase is written on by looking up and *seeing* the music or script.

❖ If visualizing a speech or script, see the opening lines of each page and know what information is in every paragraph, and where that paragraph starts on the page. Photocopy your music or script. Highlight in colors certain themes, ideas, recurring phrases, etc. Look at this color-coded page held up and to your left, then close your eyes and visualize exactly what it looked like, complete with the color coding.

❖ For musicians, away from your instrument, sit with the music closed or covered in your lap. Look up and to the left and imagine every page of the music. Read the music (off of the remembered image in your mind) and imagine yourself playing the piece. If you cannot visualize a part, open the music and hold it up and to your left to "photograph" that page into your memory. Then look away from the music and recall every detail.

❖ For speakers or actors, using colored pencils or markers, draw a diagram that illustrates key points of every paragraph. Making these in color is most effective, and keeps this visual reminder with your script or speech. Much like the above suggestion for musicians, sit quietly in a chair and envision this visual reminder in the air. If you cannot remember one part, hold the page up, look at it, then put the page down and try to see the picture in the air.

❖ Beginning at least several days before the performance, write out onto manuscript paper, the opening notes of each important musical phrase from your memory. If you cannot remember a part, simply look at the music and then close the music and write it out. In the case of a speech, write out the opening sentence of each paragraph. In actuality, this is a triple-channel exercise in itself, because you are *seeing* the music or words being written in your own hand, you are *feeling* the pen against your finger as you write, and you are *hearing* yourself say what the next note or word is that you want to write down.

The Auditory Mode

The auditory mode is accessed, as discussed in Chapter Three, by looking to the right or left, parallel with the ears. Auditory mode is very important in Triple Channel Learning, and learning to utilize the auditory mode fully is extremely rewarding. Many people have natural strategies to remember in auditory mode. For example, to repeat a phrase, name or phone number out loud a number of times is auditory programming that sound into your brain. Here are other suggestions to help you strengthen your auditory memory:

❖ Sitting at your musical instrument, practice playing through each passage, with your eyes parallel to your ears and looking towards the left. (This is easiest to do after the piece is memorized, but it is possible to do small sections as you are learning the passage). Hear the individual lines and follow where each line leads. Hear the inner notes of each chord and analyze where each note resolves to.

❖ Sing or whistle each individual line: first the melody, then the middle lines, then the bass.

❖ Sing or say out loud the names of the notes in the melody. This can be accomplished in French (solfege) or using the English names of the notes. It is important to speak out loud, and with confidence. Having implanted that auditory track in your memory, it will always remain there; much like a sound track on a multi-track recording. When you are on stage performing the piece, your brain will prompt you to hear what note to play next. What could be easier!

❖ When first learning a musical passage, *count the rhythm out loud.* Now on your multi-track recording you have a *click track* to practice with, and your rhythm will always be correct. Similarly, if you play an instrument like the harp which requires you to remember information like pedal movements, *say the name of the pedal out loud* while you are moving it as you learn the piece. That information will be permanently stored in your auditory track and will be easily accessed at all times.

If you are learning a script or a speech, it is imperative to practice saying the lines *out loud.* Use the same emphasis and tone you will use in the performance.

❖ Tape record yourself delivering your speech or presentation. Listen back and assess where you are less secure, then repeat those places over and over, five to ten times each for memory security.

❖ Role play. Speak one page of the script as if you were Will Smith, then Oprah, then perhaps a mentor or an authority on the subject that you greatly respect. Imagine you are really that person speaking, and listen to the way they might accent certain phrases to emphasize points you might have missed.

❖ Have a friend or acquaintance read the lines of your speech or script to you. This imprints your auditory memory with the *sound* of what you want to say. Another option is to record yourself and listen back to it; an invaluable tool in many ways, as you will be able to offer yourself suggestions for a better performance in addition to "hearing yourself."

For musicians, if a teacher *plays a passage* for the student to illustrate phrasing and musicality, it is much more successful than using spoken words to describe a musical sound. The student can access this auditory track and then be able to repeat it themselves much faster than just "talking about music."

The Kinesthetic Mode

Although kinesthetic is the most dangerous mode to begin a performance in, it can be a very valuable communication tool. When you listen to a profound musician or speaker, it is the *spirit* or *emotion* that he conveys in his presentation that impacts you the most. If music or speech were presented without a kinesthetic component, it would be the same as computer-generated music, or the automated voice on a telephone answering machine or computer. Certainly not memorable!

In order to have a truly moving Power Performance, the kinesthetic element must be present. It adds color and excitement and charm and enthusiasm – it adds *life*. To strengthen your kinesthetic abilities, explore these suggested activities:

❖ On a musical instrument, concentrate on how your fingers *feel* when they come in contact with the instrument. For harp, guitar, or piano, *feel* the finger on the string or keyboard, and pay close attention to the space between each finger (is it an octave, a third, etc.)

❖ Allow yourself to delve into the emotions of the piece. Practice playing a piece as if it were excruciatingly sad; then happy and joyful; then profound; then triumphant. Allow your musicality to flow, and concentrate on *feeling* the beauty of the music.

❖ For a speaker or actor, imagine exactly how the character you are speaking about would *feel* in the situation. Imagine yourself *being them.* Imagine all facets of the image. Feel the person's clothing touching your skin, imagine the air in the room, and make it all as alive as possible.

❖ If preparing a speech, alter certain visual and auditory images to be expressed also in kinesthetic terms, so you can really relate and associate with what you are speaking about. Use words like, "impacted," "jolted," and "astounded." Be brave enough to include in your speech how you really feel about certain items. Make it personal! Note that it is not a good idea to keep everything in kinesthetic terms only, as this could become too emotionally-charged to allow you to remain detached enough to maintain your equilibrium on stage.

❖ On an instrument, "press out" the tone on important phrases or melodies. While speaking, emphasize and lean into certain key phrases or concepts.

❖ Associate music you are playing, or stories you are relating, to real-life events and emotions that you have experienced. I often perform a solo harp piece which is a set of variations on a well-known theme of Paganini. In the slowest movement, which is very somber and melancholy and written in a minor key, there is one C major chord which begins the final phrase. Every time I play that C major chord, I imagine that the sun suddenly breaks through the clouds and my audience is flooded with brilliant, harmonious, glowing light. I also have super-imposed an image of my mother, who was one of the most positive and inspiring influences in my life, on that C major chord. Because of these two powerful images, I always feel a dramatic communication with my audience at that point in the piece. I realize they don't know they just got blasted with all the positive imagery I could muster, but I do know that they are aware that *something just happened!* Many times audience members will approach me with tears in their eyes after hearing this piece. A comment I often hear is, "I don't know what happened, but somewhere in that piece I suddenly realized an answer to a problem that has worried me for years!"

MAKIN' IT HAPPEN ... choose
3 of these ideas and put them into practice TODAY!

1. Using the knowledge offered in this chapter, try to figure out if you are storing your knowledge predominantly in **visual**, **auditory**, or **kinesthetic** modes. Do you find it easier to *see* the music or the speech in front of you, or to *hear* the notes you want to play or your voice saying the words, or do you instead *feel* what you are trying to communicate? Then, at your next practice or study session, concentrate on learning by accessing the mode you are most comfortable with (visual, auditory, or kinesthetic).

2. After you have an idea of what is your favored mode for learning, try to "triple channel learn" things you want to remember. Use the ideas presented in this chapter, as well as inventing your own "games" or ways to learn material in all three modes. Make

yourself use the modes which are initially less comfortable and you will realize unexpected results.

3. Before you give your next performance, plan to put yourself into visual mode before going on stage. This may take some practice . . . as you are preparing your material, get in the habit of spending a few minutes looking up, and going into visual mode before practicing your presentation.

4. If possible, videotape a performance. Watch where your eyes go and what modes you are accessing while performing. Particularly if you make a mistake or misspeak, carefully watch to see if you had delved into kinesthetic or interior dialogue mode, which triggered the problem. (Interior dialogue will be covered in depth in the next chapter.)

5. Use the power of visualization in your everyday life. Before going in to speak with your boss, or any situation which might be stressful, look up for several minutes and firmly establish yourself in visual. See if the meeting doesn't clear up things, and have a bright outcome.

6. Assist family members and colleagues to develop a built-in strategy to get "out of the dumps" and to alleviate fear and nervousness. You might want to explain kinesthetic vs. visual -- or you might simply want to steer conversation to help them see their way out of their difficulties. It is particularly important when teaching children to instill in them the confidence and knowledge that they have the power to choose how they will think and feel.

—5—

"SO I WAS TALKIN' TO MYSELF AND I SAID . . ."

The Challenge of Internal Dialogue

Internal dialogue, that little voice inside you . . . what a complex and multi-faceted element of your being! On the one hand, internal dialogue is the protector that tells you to be careful in dangerous surroundings. In many ways, internal dialogue may be a conduit to our "sixth sense." For example, if you are driving on a freeway and a car in front of you starts to swerve, your internal dialogue might say, "Be careful – that car is not safe. Pass carefully." Similarly, if you have tripped while walking on a broken stretch of sidewalk in the past, your internal dialogue may warn you to "Watch your footing. This is where you tripped before."

Internal dialogue can also be your conscience. It may say something to you such as, "Time to turn off the TV and go to bed, if I am going to get up at 6:00 am tomorrow for work!" It can also bring your attention to items that are incomplete, or need your attention such as "I need to remember to buy gas," or, "Remember to call about tomorrow's appointment." Internal dialogue is an important personal coach in everything that we do. Your internal dialogue may be telling you daily that you look good – or bad – or heavy – or skinny – or you need a haircut – that you aren't good enough, or that you are successful! It can be an important warning that something you are about to do does not seem right. The possibilities are endless. What is most important is to realize and respect the awesome power that these internal conversations have upon who you think you are and how successful you are in your life.

Internal Dialogue as Coach and Friend

When you are practicing for a performance, it is internal dialogue that serves as your personal mentor and teacher. It points out the areas that have not been learned well enough, and it serves as a constant reminder to go and work some more!

Let us look more closely at the *conversations* that occur inside your head when you are learning a script or a piece. During your rehearsal or practice times, the internal dialogue will take the form of a coach, or sometimes even a critic. It is the voice that says, "That passage needs more work," or, "I always stumble when I say that word . . . should I practice it more, or maybe say it a different way?"

Internal dialogue can be a wonderful tool when you are in the process of working to master something. It is an integral and very important element of Power Performance. It is your practice buddy, who is helping you to see where the weak parts are. Virtually anything that you have mastered in your life, from learning that a hot stove can burn you to riding a bicycle, involved endless streams of internal dialogue. Even after the activity was mastered, many people still hang on to some of the internal dialogue because they are afraid that they will forget something important if they don't keep reminding themselves.

The Intuitive Internal Voice

Let's look more closely at internal dialogue as one of your strongest links to your *instinct* or *intuition*. Because of the close link between internal dialogue and kinesthetic (they are both looking down), often internal dialogue will "voice" your intuitive feelings. You can use this connection to your intuitive self very successfully when preparing for an outstanding Power Performance.

If you listen (and feel) carefully while practicing, (be it the written word or music), it is possible to detect mistakes *before they happen*. Trust yourself, that a place which doesn't feel quite secure, or where your internal dialogue says, "watch out," is probably a place that needs more work . . . even if you have never made a mistake there before. During the creative process it is important to open up all your senses and allow your inner guide to warn you of areas which require more attention. This intuitive internal voice is one of your greatest strengths in achieving a product that is polished and secure and ready for a Power Performance.

Sometimes your internal dialogue might say, "I always make that mistake," or, "Here comes the part I can't play!" or, "I'm saying this wrong." This is not constructive. When you use the words, "I *always* make this mistake," the brain hears that as a command. How was it to know that you didn't mean it as a directive! When you allow yourself to hear a phrase like, "Yup . . . I always forget names," you are literally insuring that you always will! It would be far more productive to say, "Here is a tricky spot . . . I almost got it this time!" or, "Just about . . . I'll get it next time!"

Now going one step farther, when you come to a tricky part or phrase, say to yourself, "I *love* this part." In fact, because you

59

practice difficult passages so much in order to master them, those passages are often the most effective and perfectly executed parts of the piece in concert or presentation. So why not add an internal dialogue level into your practice of, "Great . . . here comes the part I have worked so hard on. It will be gorgeous!" All of your hard work, plus the supportive and positive internal dialogue, will assure a successful Power Performance.

One of the most freeing and powerful tools of Power Performance is the realization that because you have power over *what you think,* and *how you think,* you also have the power to alter what happens to you, to create your reality. Furthermore, how you see things, or feel about things right now, is not the way you need to think forever. It is possible to change outcomes simply by altering your view point, and knowing that you will achieve exactly *what you see yourself achieving.* A great place to start changing the way things happen for you is in *challenging* your usual internal dialogue.

There are a myriad of tricks that our mind can play on us, and becoming aware of them is a gigantic step! How often have you heard yourself say:

- ❖ "I can't play this piece."
- ❖ "I always get stage fright."
- ❖ "I will never be able to get a job."
- ❖ "He hates me."
- ❖ "I am a failure."
- ❖ "I don't know how to do this."
- ❖ "I need to introduce these people and I am going to forget their names!"
- ❖ "I have to finish my education before I can make money at this."

Challenge That Belief!

For a burst of new energy and a new "lease on life," **challenge** the limiting beliefs that your internal dialogue is sending to you. For example:

- ❖ "I can't play this piece" changes to, "I wonder what this piece would sound like if I could play it?"
- ❖ "I always get stage fright" changes to, "How do I know I get stage fright? Maybe my adrenaline is just pumping to give me more energy on stage. I can see myself looking up at the ceiling backstage, and not feeling nervous at all!"
- ❖ "I will never get a job" changes to, "How will I go about getting a job? What will I do first? What kind of a job do I want to have?"
- ❖ "He hates me" changes to, "How do I know how he feels? What exactly did he do that I might have misinterpreted? It's really silly to try to mind-read what he's feeling; he may just be having a bad day."
- ❖ "I'm a failure" changes to, "How would I act if I were successful? Actually, I do that sometimes. There are things that I am very good at."
- ❖ "I don't know how to do this" changes to, "What would I do if I knew how to do this?" or, "Who do I know that is good at doing this? Can I see myself doing what they would do?"
- ❖ "I have to finish my education before I can make money at this," changes to, "Why do I have to finish my education first? What would happen if I started working at this right now?"

By mastering our own limiting thoughts, we gain the power to be an incredibly positive influence to students and colleagues who have trapped themselves into self-limiting personal beliefs. When I am teaching, I often hear a student say to me in a lesson, "I can't do this." Instead of arguing with them (useless!), I will ask them, "What is stopping you from doing it? What would it look like if you could do it? This usually starts the student thinking in a different way and breaks the barrier that has kept him from believing he could not do something. The change usually occurs quickly because our minds are very fast to adapt to change.

Much like a trickle of water through a poorly constructed dam, once the movement of positive creative thought begins, it gains more and more energy and forcefulness, and soon it is impossible to contain. As an added benefit, the change in belief about how you perform affects your total self-belief, and all of a sudden, like the bursting dam, Power Performance has dramatically impacted all aspects of your life. Believe it and you'll see it!

Internal Dialogue and Power Performance

Internal dialogue is an important part of practicing, whether you are practicing a musical piece or practicing a speech or business presentation. And yet what is appropriate and positive in *practice* can be detrimental and negative in performance. After all, halfway through a piece on stage or a keynote speech is no time to hear your little voice say, "Help! I don't know the next part."

So, you have a conundrum. You practice privately what you want to present in public, and during that process you allow your critic or internal voice to find problems and point out suggestions for improvement. You listen carefully to the internal dialogue so you can learn thoroughly and eliminate errors. Yet when you get onto the concert stage or speaker's podium to present the material you have rehearsed, you *don't* want to hear from the "critic" who has been such an important part of the preparation process!

One Thing at a Time

There are two suggestions to overcome this problem. First, remember that the mind does not like doing two things at the same time. Internal dialogue is only one of the modes in which we store and retrieve information. Staying firmly in one of the other modes of thought will go a great distance towards keeping your internal voice out of your consciousness. If you are firmly entrenched in visual or auditory mode, you will probably **not** experience internal dialogue on stage. Should an internal conversation enter your awareness, simply switch your concentration strongly towards how the presentation *sounds* or *looks,* and the dialogue will fade into the background and lose its control over you.

Auditory and Visual are the best modes to counteract the effect of internal dialogue in a performance situation. It is possible to be accessing Kinesthetic and not have internal dialogue, but because the two modes have such a close relationship, it can be problematic. Remember that to access both internal dialogue and kinesthetic, you look *down.* This in itself forms a close bond between the two modes. Because of this, if an internal conversation begins in your head in performance, immediately access visual . . . perhaps see the music in front of you, or imagine your script in your mind – any visual image you can concentrate on. If you are speaking, see the written page in front of you, or envision an image of what you are describing. Another choice is to concentrate on *auditory;* hear the beauty of the phrase you are speaking or playing, putting energy and enthusiasm into what you are communicating. If speaking, put warmth and expression into your voice, and concentrate on the impact of your presentation. This also incorporates kinesthetic into your presentation. Any concentrated effort which stops the flow of attention towards the conversation of your internal dialogue will add to the success of your Power Performance.

Make a Deal

Another tactic is to make a formal agreement with the part of you that triggers your internal dialogue. I have used this technique for years, with great success. Before a concert, I sit quietly in the dressing room. I have a conversation with my "little voice" inside. I first tell that part of me that I know and respect that it is bringing my shortcomings to my attention for my own advancement, in order for me to become a better performer. I am extremely appreciative of this service. Further, in practice that voice has been invaluable to me and I know my music (or my speech) much more thoroughly because of the voice's assistance. However, this is the performance, and I will perform better if I do not hear any suggestions for improvement during the next two hours, (or 15 minutes, whichever the case). I make a deal with the voice that every suggestion or comment the voice has, it will put into a little imaginary black box that I carry in my head. (You can have a gold or blue box if you wish; mine has always been black.) The most important part of the deal is that I agree to sit quietly *after the performance,* either in the dressing room after I play or perhaps when I return home, and pay attention to every suggestion that my little voice put into the box during the performance. I take a piece of paper and write all the suggestions for improvement down, so that I may correct the problems the next day. This way, I still learn from the performance but the internal dialogue doesn't interfere with my concentration on stage.

Honor Your Bargain!

A word of warning: little voices are not dumb. If you break your word, and forget to listen carefully to the suggestions after the performance, (forgetting to empty the box) then this technique has less and less chance of success in future performances. You have broken the trust factor with your internal dialogue. Sometimes, even though I have set this contract up before going on stage, I still hear comments from my internal dialogue at inopportune times. It tends to be minimally disruptive, however, because I just nudge the thought towards the open lid of the black box and almost always the internal conversation agreeably ceases to bother me.

Whichever technique you choose, (or perhaps you can think one up for yourself that is personally modified), always remember *never to allow yourself to enter into a conversation with your internal dialogue when you are in performance!* Think of those extraneous thoughts or internal comments as clouds wafting across a blue sky. You will probably notice that the thought is there, like a cloud, but if left alone it will peacefully pass overhead and the sky will soon be clear and bright again..

No War

One of the most important rules of controlling internal conversation is never to engage in an argument with yourself. The last thing you want is a war going on inside your brain while you are trying to give a presentation! It is a part of human nature that there will always be a myriad of thoughts going through your brain. Thousands of pieces of extraneous information pass through your mind every minute, even every second. The trick is to allow the thoughts to pass and to not empower them with your attention. If it is worth remembering, you will think of it again. Like the beam of a flashlight, turn your attention to what you are doing or saying, and concentrate your energy on visual or auditory images. The volume of the internal thoughts will decrease and finally cease calling for your attention.

An Internal Fiasco

Imagine that you are in front of the public giving a speech. In your head you are having these thoughts while trying to keep focused on your presentation:

"The boy in the front row just opened a bag of candy. I can't believe his mother is letting him make all that noise! I wonder if I should stare down at him and embarrass him into being quiet. No, I need to concentrate on my presentation. I won't pay any attention; I'll just concentrate on what I am doing. I hate this. I can't control my internal chatter and it is going to mess me up! I am not supposed to talk back to myself. I better stop this, here comes the hard part I had trouble with in the last performance . . whoops!"

Now, replay the above scene. You are on stage and the following internal dialogue happens:

"The boy in the front row just opened a bag of candy. I can't believe his mother is letting him make all that noise! Oh – here is that important point in my speech that I really want to emphasize and put energy into. I will raise my intensity and speak (or play) louder and look up at the audience to really put this point across."

All of a sudden the disruption has been counteracted with your enthusiasm for what you are doing, and you have channeled your energy away from a possible disaster. Similarly, if it were a musical performance, after the initial thought about the boy's rudeness, you could concentrate on making the next phrase as gorgeous and beautiful sounding as any music you play in the whole concert. Dive deeply into the sound and feel of the music, and become absorbed in what you are presenting, not in the outside disruption. Imagine a golden light bathing the audience, so intense they cannot be distracted by the extraneous sound. Now you have taken a potential train wreck and turned it into a high point of the presentation. Bravo!

Internal Dialogue and Self Esteem

Of all the things you have control over, making your internal dialogue into a strong ally can be one of your greatest achievements, and an important step in mastering Power Performance. Many of the thousands of thoughts that your mind has every day are *repetitions of previous thoughts.* These thoughts and internal conversations greatly affect what we do, and how we feel about ourselves. It is fascinating that even the ones that don't serve us, often keep re-occurring. So, if they keep coming back, it extremely important to change those thoughts – "tweak" them – to ideas that will propel you forward instead of holding you back.

Think Differently

What would happen if you really listened to your internal dialogue, and when an idea was presented that was not constructive to you, which was depressing or failure oriented, you challenged this misconception and altered the way you thought about your options. Consider the internal dialogue, "I am not good enough to do this." Upon hearing that, I recommend you say, "But I am sure there are parts of this project that I have done many times before. I will do what I can, and then see how difficult the whole project looks after I start on it." Another successful challenge would be, "What would it feel like if I *were* good enough to do this? How would I know I was good enough? I will pretend that I am good enough, and have the tools and confidence to succeed, and proceed as if I know what I am doing." Just the realization that your success is greatly affected by the way your mind processes the information, and how you view the challenge, can be life changing.

It's really not what comes at you in life that is the challenge, it is how you choose to process the information, and how strong your strategy and determination is to succeed no matter what. Starting right now, I want you to decide to truly enjoy working with your internal dialogue, making an ally out of that part of your mind, instead of an enemy. Look upon this opportunity as a chance to cement a very important friendship, one that will never let you down. You will become your own best friend. Imagine how that will feel, having your inner support team with you at all times.

We can never have complete control over what happens to us, but neither can anything on the outside have control over *how we process* what happens to us! How we feel, and how happy we are, is between you and your own thoughts and internal conversations. If you establish a habit whereby the internal dialogue you hear is always presenting alternative options and creative "what if's," as well as helping you to see, hear *and* feel all of the opportunities life has to offer, what a joyous experience each day will become. In all of your everyday experiences, as well as in your performances, you will be able to follow the advice of Joseph Campbell author of *The Power of Myth*, to "follow your bliss."

MAKIN' IT HAPPEN ... choose
3 of these ideas and put them into practice TODAY!

1. For one full day, become extremely conscious of your internal dialogue. At first, just notice it. Does your internal dialogue tend to use words which present images, sounds or feelings?

2. After becoming more conscious of the internal dialogue that you experience on a daily basis, pay attention to any "universal quantifiers" that this voice may be using. A universal quantifier is an all-inclusive term that does not allow for any exceptions. Examples of this would be words like: "never, everyone and always." Challenge these suppositions with comments such as, "why not" or "maybe I can."

3. When you hear yourself say, "I always do that," challenge that statement by thinking, "Always? No exceptions ever? Every single time? What would happen if I did it differently?"

4. Notice words such as "have to, can't, couldn't, and shouldn't". These are termed "modal operators" in NLP. When you hear your internal dialogue saying one of these words, challenge your belief by saying, "What prevents me from doing that? What would happen if I did or didn't do it?" This is a fabulous way to get un-stuck in your thought processes, opening up unlimited possibilities.

5. As you are in communication with colleagues, family members and students, take notice when they express a belief that is limiting. Get them to see past their "brick wall" by using some of

the challenges listed in this chapter like, "What prevents you?" "How do you know that?" It may be particularly helpful to respond in a visual, auditory or kinesthetic mode that is in rapport with the way that they have expressed their problem.

6. Think back over a recent performance. Re-create the performance in your mind. See, hear and feel all of the things that you experienced in front of the public. Now re-examine the internal tape and remember if you were having any internal dialogue. The next step is to "edit" your memory. Watch the performance again in your imagination, but this time when the internal dialogue starts, use one of the tools from this chapter to short-circuit that thought's power over your performance. For example, the moment the disruptive thought begins, concentrate your energy on a visual image, or how the music (or speech) sounds. Notice how freeing it is to realize you do not have to listen, or even register internal dialogue. Much like a spoiled child craving attention, if none is forthcoming your internal dialogue will soon give up making a fuss!

7. Since the goal is to eliminate negative or unproductive self-talk in performance situations, it makes a lot of sense to *practice* the strategies before going on stage. Create *practice performances,* setting everything up the way it will be on stage, even the elimination of internal dialogue. This might be a great time to use the "black box" technique described earlier in this chapter, so that you can still learn from any mistakes you make.

8. It is possible to *prompt* certain types of internal dialogue. Like everything else, this must be practiced enough to become a habit. One type of internal dialogue that I have "grafted" into my thinking process is the phrase, "It would be fun to . . . " instead of, "I have to" or "I should." For example, an old model of my thinking process would be to think, "I *have to* learn that piece for the next concert, and I only have seven more days." A new and much more successful way of achieving the same goal is

first to think of something in my last practice session or performance that I really enjoyed. Then I say to myself, "It would be fun to run that great passage that I played so well . . . and then I could practice the new piece I get to play next week, and work on it until it sounds as good." Often I don't even need to take time to really play the first variation; simply by accessing the memory of performing it well, I am in a state of mind to achieve that same positive result with the new section. Notice how you can come up with a motivating phrase that encourages you to enjoy a task that you want to accomplish. Experiment with phrases such as, "I really want to" or, "I'm looking forward to . ." Keep working with these phrases until it becomes a habit to look forward to achieving your goals.

–6–

WHEN YOU THINK YOU KNOW IT...

Doing Your Homework

At the workshop on Excellence in Performance given by master teacher, Michael Colgrass, mentioned previously, I offered to be the "guinea pig" to illustrate concepts of Neuro Linguistic Programming and ways to develop an ideal mental space for performance. I knew of the importance of controlling my self doubt, internal dialogue, etc. and I made sure I was strongly in visual when I went to perform. I studiously avoided internal dialogue and my "mind set" was in an optimum performance space.

I walked up to my harp at the front of the room and began to play, expecting perfection. Then disaster happened. Half way through the piece I forgot what the next chord was . . . a mental blank! I recovered as best I could but I felt terribly disappointed with how I had played. Despite all the perfect mental work, and what I considered an ideal performance attitude, I still had a "memory slip" and made a mistake on stage. I was floored. After the performance I went up to Michael, indignant that I had made a mistake on stage *even though I did everything I was supposed to!* I will always remember his answer. He said, "You probably didn't know it well enough." How profound!

All of the suggestions in this book are designed to assist you to perform at a higher level of excellence than ever before, and with less stress. However, there is no alternative to thorough preparation. In fact, *knowing* that you have really done your homework gives more self-confidence on stage than all the NLP or Performance Practice concepts in the world.

Later, on the other side of the world, I found myself sitting next to a middle-aged woman at a reception following a concert I gave in Tokyo. She was not a professional harpist, but she deeply loved music and practiced the harp several hours every day. She was very understated and humble. At one point in the conversation she summed up beautifully what we all know inside, with the words, *"You know, I perform better when I have practiced a lot."*

The Essence of Preparation

Most people have an established procedure for learning material, and that pattern has remained unchanged for a long time. Unfortunately, we almost always attempt to learn something in exactly the same way that we have learned it before, and often get the same disappointing results. As you read this chapter, I would like you to paint yourself a new picture of how you prepare and learn. It is truly in the preparation that you ensure your success.

We all know how difficult it is to remember something that we have heard or seen only once. Take for example a telephone number. If you heard it once in passing, it would probably not "stick." If you repeat it over and over to yourself many times, and perhaps write it down, the added repetitions of the information makes it far easier to remember. This is a basic truth: that the more any information is repeated, the easier it is to recall. This is true for words in a script, for notes in a musical passage, for remembering peoples' names – everything.

In addition, the material will be learned *faster* and *more thoroughly* if there is a shorter time sequence between the repetitions. If you play a passage or memorize a paragraph of a script on one day and then play it for the second time the following day, little of the information will have stuck in your mind, and you will need to re-learn the same material. If, however, you were to play a passage or repeat a phrase or an introduction *ten times in a row,* correcting any errors between repetitions, you have a much higher chance of being able to play or recite that part perfectly the following day.

The Ten Times Rule

The Ten Times Rule is a very important concept and one that can, by itself, make a dramatic difference in your daily success with Power Performance. The mind **needs** to have material repeated a minimum of **ten times** before it is able to remember it well enough to access it under pressure. Knowing that principle, how easy it is to take the time necessary to repeat each piece of information that you need to remember ten times. It seems surprisingly simple, but the establishing of this one learning habit can have an immediate and far-reaching effect upon your success in every walk of life. Put another way, are you willing to take the chance that you **won't** be able to remember something important, when it is so easy to ensure that you **will** be able to?

The habit of repetition is easy to develop, but because it is so simple, you will need some help establishing it as a part of your normal learning strategy. Below I have listed some options to help you incorporate this simple principle into your day. Use these ideas every time you encounter something that you want to "stick" in your memory. When you read this list, mark the methods that you can see yourself doing, and that you agree to incorporate in the following week.

❖ Take a sticky note and put it on the page you are reading or studying. On this note, put a reminder to **repeat each concept ten times.**

❖ If you are practicing music, put ten pennies on the stand. Every time you repeat a passage, move one penny from one side to the other. This is wonderful for teaching students. In every foreign country I visit, I bring home a handful of exotic coins that I give to my younger students. This makes the process all the more special for them.

❖ Keep a piece of scrap paper and a dark pen beside your script, music or book that you are studying. Each time you repeat a passage, make a short line or check. I prefer two groups of five. There is a great deal of satisfaction looking at a sheet filled in with lines (messy as it may get!) and realizing that you have really concentrated, and done the repetitions that will ensure your success. That alone allows a security to develop that ensures a positive outcome.

Cut It Down!

The length of the material, or the amount of information that you try to memorize at one time, is also of paramount importance. Smaller pieces of information, learned very thoroughly, will result in a much more securely memorized final product than larger chunks of material. Imagine for a moment a pyramid in Egypt. First, see a pyramid that is made out of three very large carved pieces of stone, placed on top of each other. Now, for the second picture in your mind, envision a pyramid made of thousands of tiny bricks, all cemented together. If a huge force was to strike both of the pyramids, the one made of several large pieces would immediately topple over or be dislodged, as one piece was knocked out of alignment. The other pyramid, made of many integrated tiny pieces, would be able to withstand much more force, and if hit, the pyramid would withstand the pressure with only a small area being affected. The pyramid built of tiny pieces would still be standing.

Exactly the same thing happens in your mind when you memorize. If you have allowed yourself to clump together all of the notes or words on a *whole page*, you are taking a very dangerous risk. Like the unstable bigger blocks of the pyramid, under stress the large blocks of memorized material will fall apart. Also, having completed a large section of material, there is very little "bridge" to the next chunk of information. If nervousness or adrenaline causes you to forget any portion of your presentation, so much material has been stored together that a major memory failure will occur, making it very difficult to regain your equilibrium and continue the performance. Now, in contrast to that, imagine that you had solidly learned a much smaller section of information, such as four measures of a piece or two lines of a script or speech. That small amount of carefully learned material corresponds to one of the tiny blocks of the second, better-constructed pyramid in the earlier example. If you methodically add one small block of information after another, securely anchoring it into the larger picture with visual, auditory and kinesthetic learning, you will have a product that will be so securely represented in your mind that the presentation of it to the public will be a joy rather than a something to be concerned about or feared. You will be well on the way to perfecting Power Performance!

Short Term/Long Term Memory Insurance

Our learning process is divided into two areas; **short-term memory** and **long-term memory**. If you were to hear or read something just once, the information would get stored in the front lobe of your brain, in *short term memory*. Aptly named, short term memory allows us to access information for a very short time, for example looking up a phone number in a telephone book and remembering it long enough to dial the call. Remembering that same number a day or two later would be much more difficult if not impossible.

If you were to repeat the same information many times, the information moves from being stored in *short term memory* to *long term memory*. Just as the name suggests, this information can be accessed over a much longer time span. The more times you reconfirm the information, the longer it will be stored and the easier it will be to retrieve it. By doing a minimum of ten repetitions of every piece of information you want to remember, like writing down the number or reciting it many times, you are transferring the knowledge from short-term memory to long-term memory.

Patience and Discipline

Sometimes you might repeat a musical phrase or written paragraph ten times and think that you "have it," but come back to it the next day finding that the information is no longer available to you. Don't become frustrated . . . this is totally natural and to be expected. Simply re-learn the section the same way you did in the beginning. It will probably take less time the second day, because that information is already stored in your long-term memory. You are just reconfirming information which has already been entered into the long term memory bank of your brain.

For ideal learning, I recommend taking the smallest logical amount of material (for example, four measures in a musical piece or several lines of a speech), and repeating that small amount of material ten times *without error.* If you make a mistake in a repetition, don't count that attempt, but you don't have to start your ten repetitions over again. Just learn from the mistake and count the next perfect repetition. After learning one section, proceed to the next section, practice it a minimum of ten times, and then glue the two sections together. Make yourself say or play a whole page or entire section of the speech or musical piece five to ten times before going on to new material. Of course, you are Triple Channel Learning all this time, paying attention to how it sounds, feels, and looks.

Now you have many small chunks of material that you know very well. They are all glued together into a long ribbon of memorized material. But add into the mix the ever present element of human error and no matter how hard you prepare, mistakes can happen in performance. I am reminded of the phrase, "If it were easy, everybody would do it." So, what happens to your long ribbon of information if it gets cut? How can you regain your place in the actual performance so quickly that the audience will never know?

You have probably experienced the natural inclination, after having made an error in a performance, to go back to the beginning and start again. This is because you are so familiar with the opening (because of having started there so many times), that it seems safe and familiar. What if you had that same level of security at strategic points throughout the whole piece or script? If you had a choice of thoroughly learned "beginning places" within the body of the music or speech that you knew as well as the opening material, you would be much more successful.

Repair Points

We have already emphasized the importance of memorizing and remembering small pieces of information instead of large chunks. To facilitate this in your preparation, it is invaluable to use the concept of a **Repair Point.** A Repair Point is a place where you can begin, often in the middle of a musical section or a written paragraph, with the same security and ease that you have with beginning at the start of the piece or speech. In French, these "beginning places" are called "point de repére," hence the term "Repair Points." A professor of harp in Paris, Henriette Renié, was one of the first pedagogues to emphasize the importance of learning this technique.

Appreciating the importance of having starting places scattered throughout your presentation is easy. Think of your presentation, be it a speech or a musical piece, as a long piece of thread. In the traditional model, you would begin at one end of the thread and work your way to the other end. If something happened in the middle (your worst nightmare) you would be totally lost and needed to go back to the beginning to find your place. Now, by using Repair Points, your presentation does not resemble a long thread but instead resembles a myriad of small pieces of thread, each beginning a bit before the end of the next one. Should the thread break in the middle (the memory slip) you have a new beginning very close at hand, with minimal confusion as you begin at the start of one of the smaller pieces of thread. Often, the security of knowing that you can instantaneously recover in times of trouble is enough security to keep you from making the mistake in the first place!

Learning to build Repair Points into your preparation is very easy. It does, however, require a bit of discipline to make Repair Points a habit. Right now, as you learn the procedure, make a personal commitment to immediately include this tool into material you are working on.

First, let's examine ways to put Repair Points into music. On any given piece of music you are learning, choose the start of a phrase or pattern, every four to eight measures, and use the beginning of the melody line or section as the place for a Repair Point. This probably means you have four to six Repair Points per page, or more if you play a one-line instrument such as flute or violin.

In a script or speech, make a Repair Point for each concept or area of information you are presenting. The Repair Point will undoubtedly be one of the places from which you started your ten repetitions. Because you need to be able to start from that Repair Point with the same ease as starting at the beginning of the piece, always practice starting from that point by accessing it from your memory, not from looking at the page, or script.

Mark It

Because of the importance of our visual memory, it is necessary to make a visual cue in our music or script to mark these Repair Points. Come up with your own shorthand symbol that reminds you that this is one of your Repair Points. I use the letter R (for Repair Point), and I always mark this in a colored pen or highlighter. This way, when I am visually recalling what my music looks like, I see colored Repair Points every few lines. The dark or vibrant color helps the image stick in my visual memory. Often, I will number the Repair Points **per page,** to help me keep my place in the "map" in my head. I recommend a similar marking at the beginning of a "Repair Point sentence" in a script or speech. For an instrument as complicated as the harp, it is imperative to also include a pedal diagram for each Repair Point, and for other musicians, to include any other information you would need to make an effortless jump to that place if you were having difficulty in a performance. This second layer of stored information, the knowledge of your five or six Repair Points for each page, serves as a safety net when you are performing. If a mistake happens that "throws you off," or if a memory slip occurs, it is possible to jump to the nearest Repair Point without breaking the flow of the piece. You will be able to continue your performance with confidence and assurance. The audience need never know.

In all likelihood, you will not even need to use the Repair Points you have worked so hard on because *if you feel confident enough in your preparation, problems usually will not occur*! Susann McDonald, a famous harpist who first introduced me to the concept of Repair Points, once performed a recital in Philadelphia which I had the honor of attending. Because I had performed many of the pieces she was playing and knew them intimately, I paid close attention to each Repair Point as it passed by. Greeting her backstage after a note-perfect recital, I lamented, "What a waste of Repair Points!" She laughed at my mistake. In fact, the Repair Points were so solid in her mind that she didn't *need* to resort to using one. Therefore, they were extremely successful for her. What an admirable goal for us all to strive for!

Repair Points That You Can See, Hear, and Feel

The bottom line is that if you have Repair Points, and have repeated each of them a minimum of ten times in practice, you most likely won't ever need them in performance because your presentation will proceed flawlessly. Now imagine that those Repair Points were solidly accessed through visual, auditory, and kinesthetic modes, (Triple Channel Learning, as discussed in Chapter four of this book). If you do learn the material and the Repair Points in all three modes, I can guarantee you will perform *everything* with a confidence greater than you ever imagined. You will be ready to give a successful and dynamic Power Performance every time you are in front of the public. This achievement can have far-reaching implications on many other aspects of you life.

Security Blanket on Stage

Repair Points will become like an invisible security blanket that you always have with you when you are under pressure. To better comprehend the power of this tool, let's use the metaphor of driving a car. Imagine that you are driving into Los Angeles on Highway Ten. It is your first time to drive into this huge city, and you feel overwhelmed by the complex freeway system. You look ahead and see that three freeways intersect and you are unsure what lane to be in. Your stress level rises. You have no idea if you are on the right road or completely lost. You feel confused and bewildered. Finally, you see a sign by the side of the road that tells you that you are still on Highway 10. Whew! Each time you spot another Highway 10 sign you feel more and more comfortable that you are doing just fine and there is nothing to be concerned about. Your stress level drops and you can begin to enjoy the experience of the trip.

Repair Points serve exactly the same purpose as highway signs. They are a confirmation that you are on the right path and proceeding perfectly. They also serve as a safety net, and you know that if you do make a slip you will be able to correct it quickly and get back on track.

Put this tool into practice immediately. As you learn your next page of music, or work on your next presentation, or study for an exam, make sure to have a colored pen with you. At appropriate intervals, make a mark that identifies to you that this is a Repair Point, a place you will become so familiar with that you can begin there on a second's notice. Practice starting from that spot ten times. Now, after completing a page, go through from the beginning *only starting at the Repair Points, and only allowing yourself to play or say a tiny bit,* just enough to establish where you are. If you play too much you cheat yourself by forecasting the next beginning place. Then jump to the next Repair Point. It helps if you are numbering your Repair Points by the page, so that in your mental practice away from the instrument you can think, "page four, Repair Point three" and be able to visualize where it is, how it sounds, and notice how the music or speech feels at that point.

Think how quickly and effectively you could review a 15-minute solo or speech, going through and just playing or saying the Repair Points. This is called *chunking,* where a large body of material is chunked down to smaller sections to be more easily and securely remembered. These chunks of material are like the framework of a building, the firm foundation upon which all of the other layers can be built.

Never, Ever Stop In Performance

Have you ever been at a performance where the musician stopped in the middle of a piece, or a speaker groped in silence for the next word? Or said, "Oh, sorry – I forget what I was about to say." In the whole performance, that one intense, uncomfortable moment made a far greater impact upon you than all the beautifully executed phrases that you heard put together. Music and speech are both forms of communication, and it is unacceptable to allow the communication to be severed by stopping in the middle, no matter what happens!

I remember once performing a solo harp recital in Holland, for a prestigious audience of harpists from around the world. In the middle of one of my most difficult pieces, the middle string on my harp broke; a string that was central to the piece. Instead of ending abruptly, I improvised a new ending, working around the broken string, as if nothing untoward had happened. The audience reaction was fantastic. I had averted disaster, and had not disappointed my audience who were in rapport with my performance. Simply stopping would have made them acutely uncomfortable and unfulfilled, since music is a participatory event and we must take the audience's feelings into account.

Your new tool of imbedding Repair Points into your work, and your ability to jump to a Repair Point when necessary, will ensure that you never need to stop in the middle of a performance. However, it is naïve to think that you will keep going in a performance if you allow yourself to stop in your practice every time something unexpected happens! With the same discipline that you used to first learn the piece, or memorize the speech, you must practice the actual *performance* of that material and never, ever, allow yourself to stop when you make a mistake.

Practice Performances

The most effective way to discover any weaknesses in material you have prepared for performance is by using the following method.

- ❖ Play through the whole piece, or recite your speech from memory. No matter what happens, do not stop! Recover as best you can, and continue on. This practice performance should represent, in every way possible, the real performance. If that causes you to feel some nervousness, all the better! The more you experience performing under pressure, the better you will become at minimizing its influence upon your performance.
- ❖ After finishing the performance, take a pen and a piece of paper. Looking through your script or music, write

down every place that was at all problematic. The more detail-oriented you can be in analyzing where the problem occurred, the better. In fact, try to scan your memory to see where a problem might occur in the future or where you were at all uncomfortable and insecure. Mark these areas as potential problem spots and work them the same way as the real problems. You might have anywhere from five to twenty-five problem areas on your sheet of paper when you are finished, and the list from a musical performance might look something like this:

- *page one, line two, bar three . . . don't know the chord*
- *page three, Repair Point two, wrong dynamics*
- *page four, line one, bar two, memory slip*
- *page six, last four measures, rushed tempo*

For a practice performance of a script, your list might look like this:

- *page one . . . forgot to thank Mr. _____ for invitation to speak*
- *page one, paragraph three . . . wrong city.*
- *page two . . . bad transition into paragraph three.*
- *page four . . . too boring! I need to get more enthusiastic here, to make my point.*
- *Ending . . . practice the last two lines more so I really nail the punch line*

Be really tough on yourself! As you re-live your performance carefully in your mind, (and perhaps look at the music or script as you recall what you just did), remember to list not only every mistake you made but also any places that felt uncomfortable, where a mistake might be hiding until future performances. Having pinpointed the problems, it is amazing what our subconscious mind can do to correct the difficulties, even when we are not consciously aware that the problem is being handled.

Remember the importance of visiting material many times in a short period of time. To have a successful Power Performance means that you must study this material again *the very next day*. When you do, begin your practice by working the list (see above) that you already wrote out, containing every problem area that needs work. Here is how you should proceed:

- ❖ Go directly to the area referred to on the first line of your list. This means, start at the Repair Point in the piece or script where the problem area is, not from the top or beginning. This in itself requires discipline. Congratulate yourself for going right to the difficulty. Think of all the time you have saved.
- ❖ Correct the problem (clarify the right way to do it in your mind and then physically repeat it ten times, until it is perfect). Then, practice the whole Repair Point a minimum of ten times without mistake. Keep track of the ten repetitions, and don't cheat yourself.
- ❖ *CROSS IT OFF YOUR LIST!* It is important to make a clear statement to your subconscious mind that you have corrected the problem, and the problem does not need to continue to be of concern to you. Take a pen and cross off the offending item, and wipe the possibility of a problem in the future completely out of your mind.
- ❖ After you have worked on every item on your list, do another performance of the entire piece, or a whole recital, or your whole presentation, keeping track of any difficulties you encountered after each selection. Make another list, and work this new list the following day. As

you hone your skills to perfection, the lists will grow shorter and your confidence will skyrocket.

Success Anticipation

You will see that the size of your list shrinks each time you make one, as you correct more and more of the problem areas. By working in this way, you are only spending time on the areas that you have trouble with, and you are not wasting time practicing the parts you know. That means you will practice less and achieve more – as well as eliminating the possibility of injury or overuse syndrome. You will have more time and less pain! As you become more and more efficient with your practice time, you will develop a *Success Anticipation*: that you have done it right in the past and so the next performance will be excellent. You are building a picture of success for yourself that you carry with you onto the concert stage. You have built that picture one element at a time and it will never let you down. You will learn more about Success Anticipation later in this book. For now, start expecting awesome results and see what happens!

MAKIN' IT HAPPEN ... choose
3 of these ideas and put them into practice TODAY!

1. **Record a performance of your piece or speech. As you listen back to the recording, watch in your music or script to discover any mistakes that you may be making. Some, such as dynamics in music, you may not even have been aware of until you heard them while not playing. Write a list of all the places you want to work on before your next practice performance.**

2. **Put ten pennies or coins onto your music stand or in a convenient place next to your practice area. As you do one repetition of a paragraph or musical phrase, move a coin to the opposite side of the stand. This is a particularly effective way to have young students develop excellent practice habits.**

3. **Often it is helpful to *see* exactly where you are with your repetitions. A practice log like the one included is a visually rewarding system which helps you establish strong practice habits. This log requires that a check mark be placed on the form after each practice repetition. The advantage to this method is that it shows clearly all the work that has been done. Since some instruments, like harp and piano, require working each hand separately before putting the hands together, I have included a special form for these instruments. I recommend photocopying this before you write on it so you always have a master copy.**

Area to work:	1	2	3	4	5	6	7	8	9	10
Piano or harp:										
Area:										
RH alone:										
LH alone:										
Together:										
Area:										
RH alone:										
LH alone:										
Together:										
Area:										
RH alone:										
LH alone:										
Together:										
Area:										
RH alone:										
LH alone:										
Together:										
Area:										
RH alone:										
LH alone:										
Together:										

4. During your practice performances, *do not allow yourself to stop*! Continue through to the end of the piece and then go back and write the problem down on a list, or work on the trouble spot at that time. Get in the habit, starting now, of including a performance at the end of every day's practice of as much of the piece or speech as you have prepared. You are establishing a performance habit of not even considering stopping; a habit that you will be grateful for when you are in front of the public!

5. Invent a mark for yourself to use in your work, to indicate where your Repair Points are. Begin putting them in the material you are learning today! One ingenious student of mine invented the image "Rx," because she saw these places as a "prescription for success." Remember that by using a colored pencil or pen to mark the spots, it is helping to solidify them into your visual memory.

6. After you have written the Repair Points into a piece or script you are working on, practice going through the piece page by page, starting at each of the Repair Points. Only play or say a short portion of the area so you are rehearsing the repair point only, not making a segue to the next Repair Point. Have someone quiz you on a piece you have memorized, by asking you to begin from memory at different Repair Points. You will be astounded at the security you feel when you know your music or script this intimately.

–7–

POWER PERFORMANCE TIMES TEN

In the Beginning . . .

When I was very young (playing saxophone in my father's jazz band at age four), my parents would constantly invite people into our living room to hear me perform. I was exceptionally well schooled about the importance of those performances and the professional behavior that was expected. I always had several pieces that were performance ready, and knew that graciously introducing the pieces and "entertaining my audience" was a basic requirement of life. When I was older and traveling to different cities to give concerts (we are talking "old" as in 12 – 14), I have vivid memories of my mother going out into the hallway of the hotel we were staying in, no matter what the city, and asking total strangers if they would like to come in and hear a piece on the harp. Talk about being performance ready!

My father was convinced that all the children of the community needed as much performance experience as possible, so he formed a jazz band at our local church. Sunday mornings our group of five to ten young musicians would start at the Presbyterian Church and play the first service, then pack up and perform at the Catholic Church, then on to the United Church and so on, playing at four or five different churches or meeting halls, offering music to anyone who would listen to us. Every performance became easier. The stage, or auditorium, or school gymnasium or football field, became a second home. We got to the point where nothing could surprise us, because we had dealt with so many unusual circumstances, and still performed at our highest level. With a regime like this, it didn't take long for any fear of performing to go away.

Scared of What?

If you appear in front of the public often enough, and especially if you are fortunate to begin the process before anyone tells you it is difficult, the concept of being afraid of performing never becomes a part of your scenario. More important for me is that the joy of performing in front of people that was fostered in those early performances has never gone away and, in fact, has become stronger as I experience the joy of communicating with audiences around the world. I cannot emphasize enough the importance of having your children, acquaintances and students learn at the earliest age possible how to meet the public and "perform" without embarrassment, nervousness, or self doubt. And the fastest way to achieve that is to do it *a lot* and, following guidelines in this book, develop your own sure-fire brand of Power Performance.

The value of Power Performance was made even more crystal clear when, as an adult, I began touring for Columbia Artists Management, one of the most respected management agencies for musicians in the world. A typical concert tour would consist of 15 to 25 solo recitals, often seven or eight in a row without a night off, and all in different cities. I would always start the tours as practiced and prepared as possible. Yet, every time that I got to *performance number ten* of the tour, my performance standard altered dramatically, and very much for the better! It was as if the concert magically shrank from a "big deal" to something small and manageable. A long and complicated story magically became condensed into one simple and elegant thought progression. The challenges of the concert were minimized and the joy of performing became magnified. My creative expressiveness was able to flourish because I had, as they say, *"been there, done that"* so many times.

Ten is the Magical Number

I don't really know why every presentation gets easier and better at the tenth repetition. It is as if there is some rite of passage that must be traveled through to achieve our own highest standard of performance excellence. I can guarantee, however, that if before your next important performance you set up ten opportunities for yourself to *live the event,* under stress conditions that are as similar as possible to the final performance, that your end product will achieve a standard of excellence, that will astound you. For a business person this might be giving your upcoming sales presentation to neighbors, family, co-workers or anyone you can cajole into listening to you. Even giving a performance to a tape recorder is an invaluable experience as long as you make it as real as possible and don't allow yourself to stop during this practice.

Because of my firm belief in the value of these pre-performances, all of my university students are required to give ten pre-performances before they are allowed to perform their graduation recital, whether it is for a bachelors, masters or doctoral degree. It is extraordinary to watch the level of performance of the students escalate so dramatically, as they learn a myriad of invaluable things about their own performance abilities *in a real life situation.* I often receive emails or letters from students who have now become successful professionals, or who have continued their education at other schools, who say that learning the value of the ten pre-performances has been the most important element in their whole educational experience.

Real World Experiences

Below you will find examples of how people in three different performing environments used the empowerment of pre-performances to change their performing experience from one of terror and "I have to get through this," to one of joy and Power Performance.

Scene one: Mary's Music Recital

Mary is a music student at a conservatory. She is a pianist. She has memorized her music *a minimum of one month before her recital*. This timetable is terribly important, as the one month time span from completing the memorization process to the actual date of performance allows enough time for the mind to go from the posture of a *student,* cramming information into your brain, into an *artist* who is sharing their unique excellence with an audience.

Mary knew how important her graduation recital was, and knew how imperative the ten pre-performances were. She looked at her surrounding environment and the performance venues that she could contact in her city. Being paid for these pre-performances was not important, but often Mary discovered that there was an honorarium offered for her musical presentation. She played concerts chosen from the following venues:

- ❖ Retirement centers and nursing homes
- ❖ Hospitals
- ❖ Churches
- ❖ Benefits for worthy causes

- ❖ Private homes, either of friends or patrons of the arts who are usually thrilled to assist someone in their creative journey.
- ❖ Entertainment centers for apartment buildings, trailer parks, and condominiums.
- ❖ Elementary to high school music classes
- ❖ Social clubs, especially women's clubs or symphony and opera guilds.
- ❖ "Trading off" performances with other students preparing for their own upcoming recitals, and each one performing for the other.

Scene two: Jonathan's Keynote Speech

Jonathan was hired by a large company to give a keynote speech to a group of scientists who were considering moving to his city. The company wanted to relocate these professionals, and Jonathan was to point out the highlights of his city, and hopefully inspire the scientists to make the move with their families. There was a lot of pressure on Jonathan, as his own job rested upon the company relocating to his city. In order for him to learn where the natural "chuckles" and "laughter breaks" were, and to develop a pace for the presentation that flowed and maintained interest, he presented pre-performances of his speech in the following venues:

- ❖ For a professional speaker who was a social acquaintance. Jonathan met this friend at a party and simply asked if the speaker would listen to his speech and offer constructive criticism. In fact the professional speaker became so enthused about helping Jonathan that he listened to the speech a second time after Jonathan had worked on the suggestions.
- ❖ Toastmasters dedicated to assisting people become better speakers.
- ❖ The local Rotary Club

- ❖ A group of retired people who meet regularly for social and educational programs.
- ❖ A function for real estate salespeople
- ❖ Several retirement homes
- ❖ The Chamber of Commerce
- ❖ Jonathan invited ten friends over to his home for a potluck dinner . . . with the understanding that before dinner they had to be an audience for his presentation and offer constructive criticism.

Scene three: Susan's Job Interview

Susan had taken some time away from the work force, and was now interviewing for a potential job in a new city. Because she was back into an arena she had not been part of for awhile, she felt less than confident with her interviewing skills, and her ability to impress the people making the hiring decision. The pressure was on – this was the perfect job for her, so she really wanted to make a strong impression.

Realizing the importance of presenting a Power Performance interview, Susan set up the following opportunities to hone her skills:

- ❖ She set up an appointment to walk to a neighbor's house, introduce herself and have the neighbor give her a practice interview.
- ❖ She found three other people to interview her in different settings.
- ❖ She did a telephone interview. She set this up very formally, agreeing on a time for the conversation, each person clearing their schedules so as not to be interrupted.
- ❖ She videotaped a mock interview and carefully reviewed it.

❖ She volunteered to give a workshop on interview techniques to a local high school.

The result of this careful preparation was that Susan got her dream job, and is now enjoying her work. She reported that she was far more nervous on the phone than she was in the actual interview. The confidence of doing the pre-interview performances allowed her to relax in the job interview and project confidence and security, even smiling and laughing with the group interviewing her.

Make It Count!

Inherent in the success of these pre-performances is how *real* you make the experience. Wearing the clothes in which you will perform is very important, although if you are totally comfortable in the performance clothes after two or three experiences in front of the public, you can save the clothes bought especially for the big performance and substitute other apparel. Shoes are especially important. Think of the information earlier in this book, where you learned the importance of staying out of kinesthetic as you begin a presentation. You might be in an ideal visual head space backstage then as you make your entrance you feel the discomfort of your new shoes. Immediately all your senses *feel* the pain and you are deeply into kinesthetic. Very dangerous! Try to stay away from any clothing that makes you feel self-conscious or uncomfortable, because that will become evident to your audience within seconds of beginning your presentation, and actually make *them* uncomfortable as they identify with you.

It is very helpful to keep a journal of each performing experience. Not only will you find yourself realizing what you need to work more on, but as you read back over your notes from earlier performances, you will be impressed by what you have already learned. For example, as a musician the first time performing a long Theme and Variations, it may be a major accomplishment to remember which variation comes next! Ten times down the road and you have a new appreciation for how the composer wound certain themes and motifs from one variation to the next, and you have much more understanding of the piece to communicate to your audience. A speaker might emphasize certain words to foreshadow ideas that follow.

The Professionals Do It

One of the greatest comedy teams in history was the Marx Brothers. I have for many years performed with Harpo Marx's son, Bill Marx. As we toured from city to city, giving hundreds of concerts, I learned many of the techniques that helped make the Marx Brothers such an international success. An important element of that success was the discipline and dedication they had for their art. Before each major performance, they would take the show "on the road" and play, for example, in New Jersey before opening in New York. They believed that all the performances in Vaudeville helped prepare them for movies and television appearances, because of the constant experience of performing in different situations.

Carnegie Hall in Your Living Room

There is a story about a famous violinist quoted in *"Conversations With Kumi"* by Michael Colgrass which is inspirational. One month before the performance date in Carnegie Hall, New York, this esteemed artist sets a performance date in another Carnegie Hall... one he imagines in his own front room. In his mind this "pre-performance" has all the elements of the real performance. He really believes that this *is* his Carnegie Hall concert. He attends to all of the things that are important: what clothes to wear, his practice schedule leading up to the concert, his eating and sleeping patterns, and his schedule on the day of the performance.

At 6:15 the evening of the "concert" he packs up his violin and all his performing clothes, just as he would if he were heading for Carnegie Hall. He goes downstairs and out of his apartment building. He hails a taxi and has the driver go around the block, arriving back at his own apartment, which has now become Carnegie Hall. He gets out of the taxi and imagines he is going right to the dressing room, in this case, a bedroom of his apartment. He changes into his performance clothes with the same care he would before going out in front of hundreds of people. He then enters into his living room (Carnegie stage), bows to the imaginary audience and plays the first half of the concert, putting his highest effort into the performance. He takes an intermission in his "dressing room" (bedroom), and continues the second half of the concert. Following the performance, he packs up his instrument and walks out the door, "leaving the concert hall." After the performance is over, he reviews how he played and mentally decides what to work on. When, one month later, this artist performs at the real Carnegie Hall, the whole event has become far less intimidating since he has already done it!

All of us should learn from this example. In fact, The more times you set up a pre-performance with this concentration and attention to detail, the higher the standard of excellence you can expect in the real performance. With each repetition the whole experience "shrinks," becomes more manageable and less threatening, allowing you to perform at your personal best.

Everything is New Before It is Old, Hard Before It is Easy

Think of the first time you rode a two-wheeled bicycle, and compare that to the comfort you felt after several months or years of doing it. It's the same thing with the first time you drove a car, cooked a meal, started a new job, or played a new sport . . . the list is endless. In every case, the task got easier, your comfort level increased, and you became more confident and successful the more you performed. Yet, with something as important as a performance that you have spent immeasurable hours on to perfect, or a speaking presentation that could impact your career, you endanger your own success at the most critical point, by not preparing adequately. It is illogical to take this kind of chance, particularly when the alternative is user-friendly, enjoyable and guaranteed to make you more successful. Establish in your mind, *starting right now,* that you will allow adequate pre-performance preparation before your next important presentation. Simply expand your picture of the event to begin weeks or months earlier, and make the "event" not one single appearance, but a set of ten, of which the final one will be the best. Commit to knowing your material much earlier than is your tradition. For musicians, it is imperative to have all your pieces memorized a minimum of one month before the important concert. Going in front of the public without adequate pre-performance experiences is like a quarterback being thrown into the championship game without ever practicing with the team—not a viable option!

Fit It into Your Life

In order for you to experience the extraordinary empowerment of Power Performance, it is imperative to make a firm commitment to try out and incorporate the concepts of this chapter into your own life. Like everything, practice makes perfect. Start now, and don't stop until it's finished. The wonderful thing about Power Performance is that you can always do a better job, or have more joy as you perform, or impact your audience on a deeper level. Now that you have the tools, enjoy the ride! Commit now to encompassing these tools into your everyday life. Imagine how successful you will be!

MAKIN' IT HAPPEN ... choose
3 of these ideas and put them into practice TODAY!

1. Look at a calendar and see when your next performance is. It can be any time that you are in front of the public, and you feel nervous in anticipation. Circle a date *one month before*, and make a commitment to have all your material completely figured out, memorized and performance-ready by that date.

2. Never do something important for the first time! Set up ten pre-performances before your presentation. You will be amazed at the positive experiences you will have as you share your art with the public in these pre-performances. I have had many performers tell me that often one of their pre-performances was a more memorable or important experience for them than the actual performance.

3. Start keeping a list of potential performance venues. When you set up a pre-performance, keep a file with the names of the people you communicated with to arrange the event, their phone number, and any important information about the space, such as: do they have a microphone, how appreciative was the audience, etc. These contacts will be invaluable as you need to set up other pre-performance situations, either for yourself or your family or students.

4. Get in the habit of inviting family and friends to listen to practice performances. Be adamant with yourself that no matter what happens, you **never allow yourself to stop in a performance.** Another extremely important concept is that you **never berate yourself** or find fault with the performance while the audience is present. In fact, your "performance" continues until your audience leaves. How disappointing for a person from your audience who has just heard something that they absolutely loved, and that they thought was terrific, to then have you rip it to shreds. You are insulting your audience and robbing them of an otherwise wonderful experience. If it is a speech or introduction, **never break character.** Do not give side comments or apologetic disclosures. You are the professional. Be engaging at all times. Make sure every word you utter on stage is directed to the whole audience.

5. If you teach music, have your students get in the habit of performing for each other. If a student has a piece ready, have him showcase a performance for the next student at the end of the lesson. Regularly have the students showcase for their parents and encourage the parents to have the student perform as often as possible: at social functions, at church and school, when company or family members visit – virtually whenever anyone is available to listen.

6. If you have memorized a section of a speech or mastered one musical piece, practice performing that portion *a minimum of ten times.* The value of pre-performances does not begin when the whole program is learned. Instead every small piece of the whole becomes immeasurably stronger by the repetition of public performances. Painters, as well as sculptors and writers, have the advantage of being able to go over and correct any portions of their art they are unhappy with. Before the public views the final product of a visual artist or writer, many elements have been altered and "tweaked" until the artist feels the

104

product is ready for viewing. Musicians and live performers do not have that luxury. We form our art as the public watches. However, if we have practiced the presentation of our art enough times under performance conditions, we can prepare our product with the same security as an artist who can go back and do touch-ups. *The secret is knowing that we will perform it the way we have practiced performing it many times.*

–8–

SUCCESS!

Success Anticipation

One of the reasons that giving pre-performances is so powerful is the element of **Success Anticipation**. Success Anticipation refers to the phenomenon of expecting that *what has happened once will happen again in a similar way*. The ability to re-create or copy something we have done once is a basic element of human nature.

If a child touches a candle flame and burns himself, he quickly learns not to repeat that behavior. He will anticipate, correctly, that the same experience will happen again so he treats fire with more respect. If an athlete wears a certain piece of clothing or carries a "lucky" pendant and plays the best game of his life, a connection is often made to that pendant or clothing being a part, sometimes even a necessary part, of their future success. This is not without some merit, for if the athlete has strong positive affirmations associated with the article, and if he *believes* that he can accomplish great things while he has that article or wears certain "lucky" shoes, that belief will often become a self-fulfilling prophecy.

Society Provides Success Anticipation

The same phenomenon can be seen with a child who has been brought up in a well-to-do, successful family. The child sees abundance surrounding them, so they expect the same abundance in their own life. Often a high work ethic is also exhibited in the family (instrumental in providing the abundance!) and often the child will adopt a Success Anticipation that he will get good grades and succeed at whatever he decides to pursue, in harmony with the family values. It is a variation on, "monkey see, monkey do."

Modeling Excellence

Often the children of famous musicians also become outstanding artists. On the one hand it could be said that they inherited talent, and had the advantage of their parents' support and connections which assisted in the child's advancement. I believe however, that it is something much more pervasive and inherent to human nature. The child is simply modeling the behaviors that he has seen the successful parents do. First, he watched the work ethic of the parent practicing many hours daily to achieve a high level of precision. Following that preparation, when he witnesses the mother or father going on stage well prepared and confident, he is likely to follow their example. The child anticipates that he, too, will be able to go on stage and receive the warmth and enthusiasm from audiences because he has seen that natural flow of events so many times ... a built in Success Anticipation. If you have experienced yourself doing something very well, (which we all have, face it!) and especially if you have done it well more than once, then you already have established a Success Anticipation. You have an expectation that the next time you do the same thing, you will do a great job. If you have a picture, or a feeling, or can hear yourself doing an outstanding job in a presentation, or performing a piece at a very high level, and you have experienced that reality, then you have a *belief factor* that you can do it again . . . and most often, that belief will be realized.

Unfortunately, the opposite is also true. If you have had a bad experience in front of the public, there is a natural fear that that failure will happen again in the next similar situation. To remedy this problem, set up for yourself a number of smaller, less intimidating performance opportunities in which you are certain to do well. Build up your confidence gradually, making sure that you "stack the deck" by asking yourself to perform small, easily achieved tasks that you are sure to complete successfully. This gradual building up of confidence is also important in teaching. Having a child do many performances of material they are certain to do well on is imperative in helping them form positive Success Anticipation for themselves – an extraordinarily important gift which will affect many parts of their lives.

The Importance of How You See Yourself

Each of us is constantly remodeling the image that we have of ourselves and our capabilities. Based upon the successes or failures we experience each day, we form beliefs about what we might be able to accomplish in the future. As performers, it is imperative to respect the power and influence of this internal self image, for only if we believe that we can do something can we truly achieve it . . . especially in front of several hundred people.

There are two sides to this concept. The first involves Success Anticipation and the other, an expectation of failure. It is important to remember that our internal video camera is *always on*, making assessments and judgments about what we can and cannot do **at all times**. This unleashes a myriad of important and interconnected concepts, all helpful in the mastery of Power Performance.

Success Strategies

1. **Your Reality.** Realize that your reality is, and always will be, the filter through which you process the information that comes at you. Whenever you do *anything,* the way that you process and view that action *for yourself* will have a tremendous effect on how that action influences your internal picture of the world. Imagine, for example, that you are practicing an entrance for a speech or performance. You rehearse how you will walk on, bow, and begin to perform. Then you review what you have just done. At this point, you have a choice of either building a *Success Anticipation* for the next time, or just the opposite, an expectation of failure. It all depends upon how you choose to view what you have done. If your internal dialogue says, "Looks good . . . head up, posture erect, I am full of energy and enthusiasm, I came to center stage . . . and next time I can see myself smiling more at the audience." You now have a Success Anticipation that you will do all those positive things on your next rehearsal or performance, and you will *add* the smile. Another way of reacting to exactly the same scenario would be to think after the rehearsal of your entrance, "Darn! I forgot to smile again. I never remember that part. This is too hard. I will probably screw up the opening anyway." Now, instead of a Success Anticipation, you have undermined your own belief that you can do a good job. Coming from this position is far more demanding and difficult, and takes away the joy in your preparation. You will get tired and disillusioned quickly, and be less inclined to keep practicing and perfecting the entrance.

2. **Start Small.** As you are preparing for a performance, try as much as possible to ensure that you will have a positive experience. For example, if you give a number of pre-performances, start the first one by performing only a portion of the whole – and make sure to choose a part that you feel great about! As you realize that you did a terrific job on that first portion, you will develop a Success Anticipation that you will "ace" the whole performance. Gradually build up the amount of material you are presenting. After every presentation, congratulate yourself for working hard on becoming a better presenter, and be proud of your successes. Anything you did not do perfectly is just an opportunity to do better the next time.

3. **Respect the act of PERFORMING.** Never surprise your subconscious. Putting yourself under performance pressure if you have not adequately prepared is not a good idea. If you are working on mastering a piece, for example, a minimum of ten performances is essential, but make sure to know the material before putting yourself in front of the public. Be comfortable with the music (or script), and also with your own mental preparation. At least as far in advance as the night before, you must begin to build yourself a visual image of how you will look as you give a masterful performance. Build up to the event in much the same ways as an athlete does before a game or competition, with rest and focus, and utilizing the techniques included in this book. See and sense what you will wear and how you will move. Hear in your mind what you will say or play. Experience the whole video of your performance, from start to finish, in your mind. The more vivid you make this image, in color, with motion, and seeing all the surrounding environment, the more value you will gain from it and the more confidence you will have the next day in performance.

4. **All The Way.** It is important to visualize in your mind the **whole performance**. An outstanding American female athlete competed in the Olympics a number of years ago. She had prepared extensively. In the final competition she was amazed when, at the end of a perfect run, she faltered and failed to win the race. As she surveyed her mental preparation, she realized that *she had never visualized the end of the race.*

5. **It All Counts!** Take every performance seriously, no matter how large or small the audience is. Your own self-image does! Unfortunately, one negative experience can have a stronger effect on your self assurance than many positive experiences. By treating the act of performing with great respect, and always "stacking the deck" in your favor, you are helping to *build* a strong belief system in yourself. This is not to say that you should never perform spontaneously. That has great value and merit in itself, but unplanned performances must be on well-seasoned, tested and perfected repertoire that you maintain at a high professional level.

6. **A Piece in Your Pocket.** Always have material that can be counted on for a positive and impressive performance available and ready at all time. Even a relatively young musician should always have a "showpiece" memorized and ready to perform. When this piece is well received, it will help establish a marvelous Success Anticipation for the future. Similarly, a spokesperson should always have a few insightful words, a story or a joke that they can count on to present when put in front of an audience without preparation time.

7. **Leading.** This element of Power Performance is very useful when you are in conversation with someone else. It is a

variation on Success Anticipation which is also extremely valuable for teaching and coaching. Often Success Anticipation can be built into a conversation, by leading with questions that will be answered in the affirmative. First, establish rapport with the person to whom you are speaking. This is accomplished by stating things that are easily agreed upon, and which make the other person feel harmonious with you. After rapport is established there is a natural anticipation that there will be agreement to the next statement you make. Knowing this, it is possible to lead the person's thinking, to insert ideas that they might not feel so sure about. Because the mind has accepted all the previous information as true, it is willing to accept the new concept as also being true. For example, this might be a conversation between a teacher and a student:

> Teacher: "What a gorgeous concert hall this is!"
> Student: "Yes, it is."
> Teacher: "The lighting on this stage is perfect."
> Student: "Yes, I can see very well."
> Teacher: "The acoustics are terrific . . . every note you play on stage resounds through the hall beautifully."
> Student: "Yes, it does."
> Teacher: "You are going to sound fantastic here, and perform wonderfully this evening."
> Student: "Yes, I think I will!"

The teacher has established a rapport with the student, and has led the student from one verifiable statement to another, and finally to a suggestion of success, which is unverifiable but now likely because the mind has accepted the idea of success and anticipates it. The conversation between two people in this example could also have been an internal dialogue inside the performer's head, and would have had the same positive effect.

Unfortunately, the flip side of the same concept can also be very strong. One negative thought can trigger an avalanche of thoughts that lead to an expectation of failure. Imagine overhearing this disaster-infested conversation from a performer preparing for a concert:

> Performer: "I feel like I am getting a cold."
>
> "The lighting on this stage isn't what I am used to."
>
> "I feel a draft coming from the left side of the stage and my fingers might be too cold to perform."
>
> "The last time I played a concert and my fingers were cold, I had a terrible memory slip."
>
> "I really am nervous. I am afraid I won't be able to play well."
>
> "This concert is going to be horrible."

Listen carefully to your own internal dialogue and learn to channel your thoughts to give yourself the advantage of a *Success Anticipation*, not *disaster anticipation*. Both states of mind can be very powerful!

8. **Anchoring.** Success Anticipation can be made much more effective when you accompany it with a physical anchoring. In anchoring, you combine a physical trigger with a remembered experience. By doing this you can establish a unique and incredibly strong personal tool by combining the physical sensation (the anchor) with your own positive feelings about your accomplishments and potential. This tool can assist you to establish an ideal mind set before a performance, or assist you in any stress-filled situation in your life. When you feel your anchor, you will also experience all the positive energy associated with it.

❖ What you are actually doing is strengthening your own Success Anticipation; your own positive belief system about your capabilities. You are accompanying the thought with a physical activity, like pressing two fingers together or pressing your thumbnail into the tip of your second finger, as an "anchor." Work through the following steps to establish your own anchoring mechanism. As you read each step, accompany it with the action so that you can experience this important tool on a personal level. Decide upon a physical anchoring technique that is user-friendly and convenient for you. Since you are a performer, find a subtle physical action that you can do while you are on stage. Make sure it is appropriate and feels comfortable for you. Something like pressing your thumb and second finger together might be great for a singer, but ridiculous for a pianist! Pressing down with the big toe on your right foot might be ideal for a speaker (especially as that would also "ground" you), but impossible for a ballet dancer. So - the first step is to devise a simple action that you can do inconspicuously, but that is immediately identifiable to you as your anchoring device and unique to this purpose. Think of an anchor you like right now, and try it out a few times.

❖ Think about something that is incredibly special and positive on a personal level. It might be a family member, or a pet, or a favorite place in nature. Whatever it is, imagine that special thing with all your energy. Experience what it feels like to be in or around that special energy, and bask in the memory for a moment. As you do so, squeeze your fingers together, or do whatever action you have decided is your anchor. Repeat this several times. As with all exercises, experiencing the image in all three channels of kinesthetic, visual and auditory will be most effective.

❖ See yourself at some point in your life when you felt great about yourself. Imagine how you looked, and see your clothes in vivid colors. Think where you were and imagine you can feel the temperature of the room, the movement of air around you, and any aromas that may have been present. When you experience this image, squeeze your anchor point in the unique way that you have decided upon for your anchor.

❖ Remember a compliment that you received from someone you respect. Recall their words, what they looked like, what they said about you and, most important, how it made you feel. Anchor this in with your personal anchor.

❖ Imagine a physical sensation that you love. It may be standing under a hot shower, or basking in a Jacuzzi or jumping into a swimming pool or soaking in the sun. Anchor this in.

❖ Imagine yourself performing at your best. Recall a time when you were performing at a very high level, and felt extremely confident about what you were doing. Add this to your anchor by pressing or squeezing the anchor point you have devised.

Okay, you have a great start! Now, press your anchor and notice how this physical sensation brings with it all the positive energy of the experiences that you have anchored in. It is an instant outpouring of sunshine and positive energy.

As you go through the next few days, and especially as you have outstanding experiences in performance, anchor in these positive sensations to add to your stash! It is like a bank account. The more positive energy you store away, the more you can withdraw when you need it. As you are about to go into a performance or stressful situation, squeeze your anchor, and you will be immediately flooded with the feeling of your own successful experiences. This allows you to access your own highest potential at all times. Much like a rechargeable battery, the more you recharge these anchored-in feelings, the stronger the signal that you will receive back from your own personal battery of positive energy when you need it. Sometimes you may squeeze your fingers or access your personal anchor and think nothing is happening – but when you go into the performance or stressful experience, you feel positive and empowered. Your brain is accessing "you" at your best.

It is also possible to anchor in associations for others. One middle school teacher anchored an attitude of success into the pencils her students were holding. She had the students use special pencils to take a series of math tests that she was sure they would do well on. Then when the important exam came, she handed out the "special" pencils which flooded the students with memories of success and confidence.

It is also effective if a teacher presses a student's arm or shoulder as they say, "Good Work!" Pressing the same shoulder or arm later will bring back all those compliments and achievements, leaving the student anchored into an ideal mental space. If criticizing or correcting the student at another time, the teacher must be careful not to touch the same anchor because this confuses the positive reinforcement they have been establishing.

Like anything that is worthwhile, an anchoring technique needs to be practiced and used to become a habit, and to be established as an easily accessible part of your coping strategies. The more you use this tool, the stronger and more effective it will become.

9. **The Messages We Give.** As important as the messages that we give ourselves are the messages that we send to others. Remember that everyone we interact with is working with their own internal video cameras, establishing and re-evaluating their own sclf worth. There is a misconception that what is said to children is important in impacting their self-image, but that adults are sure enough of themselves that your words or actions will not have an effect upon their internal picture. WRONG! Particularly for a performer, the power of the spoken word either to assist him in building a confident and positive self-image or to destroy his belief in is extremely potent. One of the joys of knowing Power Performance and the principles described in this book is that you no longer are ignorant of the power of your words. You are now aware of the power of your words and can lead others into paths of thinking which will positively impact their lives.

The Impact of Power Performance

At my University, my students weekly perform in a Master Class, each giving a memorized solo performance in a beautiful concert hall to an audience of their peers. This allows them to hone all the techniques of Power Performance necessary for a successful performing career. One day a graduate student was slated to perform, but could not be found at the time of her performance. I searched the halls of the school and finally found her in a corridor, very upset and crying. After speaking with her a while I discovered that many years ago a famous harpist who was touring her country had heard her play and had said the words, "You can't play from memory." To be fair to the visiting harpist, this statement was very possibly a portion of a longer sentence, such as "you can't play that piece from memory yet," but regardless of the intent, the damaging proclamation that the student heard . . . and carried with her for years was the statement *that she could not perform from memory.* This was made dramatically stronger because it came from a successful performer whom the student greatly admired. The echo of these words, "you can't play from memory," set up an expectation of failure for the student that loomed in front of her as an overwhelmingly large and menacing prophesy of failure as she approached the concert stage.

By using the elements of Power Performance that are outlined in this book, I am happy to say this story has a marvelous ending. I set up a number of opportunities for the student to perform with guaranteed success, beginning with very short, easy pieces that I was certain she could play perfectly, and working up to very difficult repertoire. Each successful performance helped her set up a Success Anticipation which pre-empted the belief that she would fail. In addition, by using tools of **reframing** which will described in detail in the following chapter, we altered the way that she viewed her own potential to include a much more positive and successful picture. This student is now performing successful solo recitals in major concert halls around the world.

MAKIN' IT HAPPEN . . . choose
3 of these ideas and put them into practice TODAY!

1. **Make a commitment to find a personal anchor that is convenient for you to do while you are in front of the public. (Because of this, you might want to choose one that does not involve two hands.) Practice the positive anchoring exercise from this chapter, and then commit to anchoring in one more positive experience every day for five days. You might even want**

to put sticky notes up on your mirror or fridge, or on your schedule book to remind you to do this, until it becomes a habit. Then, before you face anything challenging, (from a dental appointment to a discussion with your boss about a raise), use your anchor to put yourself in your ideal space just before the event.

2. Become aware of conversations around you. See if the people you are speaking to are setting themselves up for success or failure. If possible, lead them into a more positive vein of thinking.

3. Listen carefully to your own internal dialogue. When faced with a challenge, do you habitually think of how you have surmounted such a challenge in the past, or do you tend to remember times that have not been as successful? An example of this is when you are looking for something that you have lost, such as your keys. One person will look in many places, surveying the rooms for the keys that they know are lost. They are sure that the keys are lost, and therefore cannot find them, (in fact, they are looking where they are certain they will not find the missing keys). A second person who chooses to use Success Anticipation will think, "I know the keys are here. I can see them sitting on that table, or behind that book, or in my pocket . . ." The second person is certain that the keys are waiting to be found, and as anticipated, the keys *will* be found.

4. In performance, when you approach a difficult or demanding passage, remember how beautifully you have performed that part in rehearsal or practice. Anticipate that it will be just as beautiful in performance. Remember to "love" it!

5. As you greet an audience from a speaker's platform or the concert stage, anticipate that they will love what you are about to present. Remember responses that you have received from other audiences (which you have programmed in to your

personal anchor) which were very positive, and expect a similar warm and spontaneous response. *Know* that the audience will love you. In fact, thinking "I love you" will have a great impact on your presentation and your success.

6. Make a commitment to yourself to establish a "showpiece" that you will always have ready to perform. For a speaker, this may be a story or narrative that you know audiences enjoy. For a musician, choose a piece (length is not important . . . in fact, shorter is often better) that exemplifies your love of your instrument, and your virtuosity. **Always** have this piece "under your fingers," ready to perform. As you store up positive reactions to your performances, you are building your personal arsenal for success.

—9—

BRAIN CHANGE

You Can Change Your World

Have you ever wished that you could change the way you think? Wouldn't it be fun to just be able to go into your brain with a magic whiteout pen and take the rough edges off some of your less-than-successful experiences? You could change the *residue* left after an event or a performance, the kinds of memories that make us all go "ouch" when we think of them. It would be possible to take a comment like "you can't perform from memory," or "you aren't good enough," or "You can't do this," and you could change the way that the comment made you feel, or alter the way you processed it, so that you felt inspired to excel rather than feel defeated. You could see your successes and failures in a different perspective, perhaps one that was less personally involved, after you had the advantage of time and experience to round out the whole picture.

Well, you are in luck! There are Power Performance tools that can allow you to do exactly that. One of the most powerful of these tools is **reframing.** The word "reframe" accurately describes what this accomplishes. It takes a picture that you have in your mind and puts a new, improved frame around it. This allows a new way to look at the same experience so that it no longer seems threatening, humiliating, embarrassing, or uncomfortable. You actually edit your memories so that you

123

see, hear and feel what happened in a new way. When seen in this new perspective, your reaction to remembering an event from your life might change from feeling queasy in the stomach to a sense of gratitude and empowerment for what you learned from it.

Consider that your brain is a computer. This computer has diligently stored away all of your experiences, complete with grammatical and content problems. Now, because of the tools in this chapter, you get to go back to all those old, outdated files and make changes. Some files, or experiences, you will want to delete completely from your inner computer. Some require only moderate changes in perspective to become positive, supportive information that will assist you in your life. The thrilling part is that you are in control of this computer. Just as you were able to input the original information, you are in control of how you want to access your memories, and the impact upon your life that you wish those experiences to have. Being able to control and edit your own life experiences is an extraordinarily empowering ability. As you rebuild and reprocess events and memories of your life, you are gently changing the way you think about yourself. You will lose much of the old, useless mental baggage that we all accumulate daily, and rework it into information that will make you stronger, more confident, and self-assured. Further, because you can reframe your reaction to anything that happens in your life, you will be less afraid of making mistakes or being vulnerable. You know that you have the power and the tools to overcome any challenge and re-assemble your cognizance of any experience. As your confidence and zest for life increases, you will be able to approach any experience, from giving a presentation or concert to any personal interaction, with the confidence and security that you will be successful.

Since every person has a unique way to process information and to experience the world, there are many different variations of the reframing concept which will appeal to a greater or lesser degree to each individual. A number of these have been outlined below. Each is a valuable technique. I recommend exploring all of the ideas listed below, then return to those that appeal to you most and incorporate them into your daily life. In each case, use experiences from your life that tend to weigh you down or be uncomfortable and depressing to think about. Why not clean out your own mental computer as you learn these important tools!

See It on TV

For this exercise, think back to an experience in your life that makes you feel uncomfortable. Maybe it was a performance that did not go well or a distressing conversation that you had that still bothers you. See the whole scene on a large-screen television set in your mind. Follow each of the steps below and at the end we will explore whether the impact of the original memory is still as strong as it once was or if your cognizance has altered. Follow these steps:

- ❖ First, see the problematic scene on a large screen television set in front of you. If there is movement in this scene, go ahead and let the scenario play out on the television screen. Make the picture as real as you can, seeing, hearing, and feeling everything that happened. Make sure to turn up the volume knob on your TV screen so you can hear clearly.
- ❖ Imagine that the television screen now grows into a massive, huge screen in front of you, maybe the size of a house. View the event again on this huge screen. See how you feel as you watch this enlarged picture. Take a moment to experience this bigger-than-life event.

❖ Now shrink the TV monitor to a very small size. Imagine that the characters on the screen are all the size of a child's doll.

❖ Bring the TV screen back to the original size in your mind. Now alter the way the picture looks. Darken the colors, and then lighten them until the screen is almost white. Move the position of the TV around in your mind, to the left and right. Add sound, and then take the sound away.

❖ After altering this picture in your mind, review how you feel about the original event. Probably the impact of the experience is much less devastating to you already.

Zoom In

❖ Imagine again your original picture on the TV screen in your mind. Watch the monitor as the following happens:

❖ The camera that is filming this scene zooms in so close that all you can see are the fibers on your shirt or sweater. Move the camera around so you see a magnified view of different objects around you. Make sure to completely experience each step of this exercise for maximum benefit.

❖ Imagine the picture from a mouse-eye view. No, don't just think it, **really do it!** See how out of proportion all the people look, when looking WAY up at them.

❖ Now zoom way out so that you see a whole block, then a whole city on the screen, and your drama is being unfolded in a very small area of the picture.

❖ Take a few minutes and experiment back and forth, changing your perspective on the event.

Now, think back to how you felt at the beginning of the exercise. Does the event still have the same impact on you? If so, continue with the same picture for the following exercise. If

126

you have dislodged some (or most) of the discomfort from that one memory, choose a different psychological "wound" from your memory to experiment with in the next exercise.

You Haul

❖ First, recall an event which troubles you. Now, see, hear, and feel the memory of this event happening on a TV set in front of you.

❖ Load the television set, which still has your picture on it, into the back of a pick-up truck with the tailgate down. Watch the picture carefully as the truck drives off into the distance. See how much smaller the picture gets as the truck moves farther and farther away, until you can barely see the truck on the horizon.

Go the Distance

❖ Pretend that you are on a mountain, several miles away from where an unsettling event took place. You can see the lights of the city and even the building or area where this interaction took place. Notice how small that building looks, let alone the image of you inside the building, in comparison to the whole city. You realize that in every other home and office, human interactions and even life and death dramas are playing themselves out. Allow this paradigm shift to alter the way you feel about the experience.

Toss It!

❖ For this exercise, remember another experience from your life that is uncomfortable. Shrink down your image of the event and place it in the palm of your hand, complete with all your associated emotions.

❖ Crumple and squish the image into a tight little ball. Have fun doing this!

❖ Now, with all your might throw the ball as far as you possibly can, imagining it is headed for the stars.

❖ Throw the ball with all your energy and as you throw it, say "Shoooooo!"
This adds an auditory element to the cleansing process. (Visual mode is already working wonderfully here, as you watch the ball until it literally disappears. Kinesthetic is involved, as you use your whole arm to throw the ball with as much energy as you can.)

❖ Repeat this process several times. Remember to say, "Shoooooo!" as you do this exercise. Doesn't it feel great to throw this garbage away? I always imagine that all the negative energy that I had wrapped up in the original memory gets recycled by the universe into productive, positive energy; plus I get the use of the brain cells that were storing the useless negative energy. I can imagine bright golden sunlight pouring into the empty cells, filling them with creativity and new ideas.

The Glass Ball

Chances are the memories you started with at the beginning of these exercises do not look or feel the same to you now as they did when you began. After all, you have crumpled them up, shrunk them to almost nothing, and tossed them to the stars. So I suggest you come up with another "yucky" image from your own personal garbage heap that you carry around inside you.

❖ Imagine that you have a fragile glass ball in the palm of your hand. It looks like a large, diaphanous Christmas

128

tree ornament. Into this glass ball, stuff the negative experience you just pulled up and all of the accompanying, uncomfortable and disruptive feelings that are associated with the scene. Stuff all this into the glass ball that you have in your upturned palm.

❖ Did you forget anything? How about any lingering nagging self-doubts or black, oozy feelings that have hung around with this memory for a long time. Throw it all in!

❖ After you have everything inside, carefully set the glass ball down on the floor.

❖ On the count of three, stomp on the glass ball with all of your might. Imagine that the force of your foot stomping down on the glass totally vaporizes everything in the glass ball, as well as the ball itself.

❖ You are now totally free of that particular ugly memory, and the wonderful thing is that the creative mind now has a lot more space to fill up with pure, golden, creative brilliance. It is like letting the sunshine into a box that has been locked shut for a very long time.

University students of mine have often been spotted coming out of a tough exam   or competition and stopping in a corner to "smash a glass ball" containing any lingering memories of "I can't do this," "I really screwed up," or "I'm a lousy performer," which were spawned during the exam or performance. This exercise can also be done very successfully with a group of people, such as a musical ensemble or a sports team.

Bury It

Recently on a concert tour to Japan, I found I was carrying around a lot of trepidation about my ability to play a certain, very difficult, piece. Intellectually, I knew this feeling was not appropriate, since I had learned the piece very well and was totally prepared for the performance. Regardless of the inappropriateness of the feeling of inadequacy, I was deep in the middle of an insecurity crisis. With a major performance scheduled for that evening, I had to do something! I decided to go for a walk in a beautiful Japanese garden next to my hotel. I found a gnarled old tree with some soft soil at its base. I searched my pockets and found I had a small amount of wadded up tissue. I took a small piece of the tissue and with all my creative imagination; I listed on the tissue all the insecurities I had about the upcoming performance. When I had completed my, "I can't do this" list, I dug a tiny hole at the base of the tree and literally buried my worries. I packed the soil down with determination. As I stood up I felt a strong sensation of cutting away any association with those concerns. They were not part of me anymore. I continued my walk in the garden allowing the beautiful Japanese sun to fill all of the dark crevices inside my mind that had just been emptied. When I went to the concert hall later that afternoon, I was truly looking forward to the performance, and my lightened heart allowed me to "ace" the concert.

There are many variations on this "burying your worries" technique. Here are some options. I am sure you will be able to add to the list with your own creative solutions. And it is okay to enjoy this process! Try these out:

- ❖ Write your worries, anxieties or feelings of inadequacy on a piece of toilet paper and flush it down the toilet. In fact, flushing is totally appropriate!
- ❖ Write (either really write or imagine writing) your stresses and concerns on a piece of paper and light it with a match. As you see it go up in flame, you realize that nothing but a bit of smoke is left; certainly nothing worth worrying about!

❖ Take an uncomfortable memory of yours, (particularly if it was a criticism) and pour that memory into an imaginary bag of manure. See all of the words of the person who insulted you flowing into the bag. Now, take the bag of manure to an imaginary rose garden. As you spread the manure around the roses, think how appropriate this is. The smelly and disagreeable substance in that bag is invaluable to the successful growing of beautiful flowers – which is just what you have done with the memory. Go ahead, *be a rose*!

One Christmas when I returned home from an international tour, I did a variation on this technique. I found a glass Christmas tree ornament. Into the center of the ornament I mentally put all the anxiety and stress from the tour. I put the ornament into a plastic baggie and with a hammer, proceeded to hammer the ornament to shreds. (Probably I had been hiding a desire to do this to a Christmas ornament since I was a child, but psychoanalyzing *that* really belongs in another book!) As I threw away the harmless pile of powdered glass, I was relieved to find that all my concerns had vanished and I was ready for a fresh start on the holiday.

Pink Garbage Bags

The inspiration for this tool came from a wonderfully spiritual person named Michael McGinty who assisted me when I was in Kansas City on a concert tour.

❖ Bring to your mind a concern that you have been harboring.
❖ Relive in your mind the experience that has plagued you, and honor all of your feelings resulting from the occasion.

❖ See each concern, worry, feeling of anger, hate, or despair that you have associated with this memory flowing into an imaginary large pink plastic garbage bag and tie up the top.

❖ Now let go of the pink garbage bag. Like a helium-filled balloon, see it rising into the sky so that the universe may recycle the energy into a more productive purpose. It is no longer your business. Feel the lightness in your soul now that you have lost this burden.

Next

I first heard about this fabulous technique from Wayne Dyer. Do each step as you read the procedure:

❖ Put your left hand out in front of you and turn your hand so the palm faces to your left.

❖ Bring to mind a mistake you made or a memory that bothers you.

❖ Place that worry on the left side of your palm. Make sure to include all our negative feelings of inadequacy.

❖ On the count of three, swing your arm to the left, pushing the memory away from you, and say "NEXT"

❖ As you say "next," purge the thought and the feeling from your consciousness. You are dismissing the thought into the PAST as you allow the FUTURE to replace that image with positive, empowering energy.

ADDED BONUS: You can do this extraordinarily powerful exercise in your head, even as you are performing! "NEXT" any wrong notes, mistakes, mispronounced words the moment they happen so your total concentration can be with the remainder of your performance.

MAKIN' IT HAPPEN ... choose
3 of these ideas and put them into practice TODAY!

1. People learn things much better if they teach the information to another person. Go through the above list and choose one or two reframing strategies. Commit to passing on this information to another person, particularly if you know someone who is having trouble dealing with a situation or memory.

2. Tomorrow, as you through your day, identify feelings, reactions, or memories that might stick with you and cause you concern. Before these memories have a chance to build up into real garbage, quietly go in a corner or quiet place, put the experience into a glass ball in your hand, put it carefully onto the floor or ground and SMASH IT with your foot. Think of it as caring for your mind much the same way as you use dental floss to care for your teeth so plaque won't build up and calcify. You are getting rid of the mental plaque that builds up as we go through life ... before it calcifies in your mind and becomes a much bigger problem.

3. Pass on the glass ball technique to a child. In many ways, a child is able to incorporate these wonderful habits for a healthier mind into their lives more easily than adults because of their uninhibited imaginations.

One of the most precious memories I have is of my daughter when she was four or five years old. She was dancing in the Nutcracker Ballet. I went backstage between performances to see how she was doing, and I found her in a corner with another young child. She was teaching the little girl (another ballerina with a tear-streaked face), "the glass ball" technique, to purge the frustrations of a mistake made in the previous performance so as to be able to go on stage and perform again with confidence.

133

–10–

REFRAME IT

Make That Change

Steven Covey, author of "Seven Habits of Highly Effective People," uses a very effective example of what he calls a paradigm shift in his public speaking appearances. He tells the story of a man riding on a New York subway, going home after a hard day at work. The man is tired and very disturbed by a family of two boys and one small girl who are on the same subway car. The boys are throwing things to each other, often barely missing the heads of the other people on the train. The young girl of about four or five is running up and down the central aisle of the subway car, screaming. Everyone on the car is upset at the unruly behavior of the children, but their father seems not to notice. He sits quietly, involved in his own thoughts, not reprimanding the children at all for their behavior.

A tired passenger can stand it no longer. He walks up to the man, infuriated that the children are being so disruptive. He says, "Can't you control your children? They are being very loud, and the girl is running all over the car!"

The father looks up and seems to have difficulty focusing. He says, "Oh, I am very sorry. I didn't notice. You see, their mother just died and we are on our way home from the hospital. I suppose they are just trying to deal with the situation."

Immediately there is a shift in the way we view the whole scene. Instead of being angry with the father for not managing his children, we now feel compassion for the family. In place of the tired commuter wanting to correct the children for their behavior, now he wants to hold and protect the family, to shelter them from the pain they must be feeling.

The situation has not changed, but the commuter's grasp or understanding of what is going on has been altered. He is processing the same information differently. This is called a **paradigm shift, or in NLP terms, a reframe.**

Make It Work for You

Often when we are frustrated with our own performance, or the way that one part of our career or life is going, a simple paradigm shift can make a huge difference. Often as I drive home from work, my mind is fretting, figuring out how to deal with some problem or personnel issue that seems overwhelming and terribly serious. Sometimes I glance up and discover that there has been a traffic accident, and my mind does an instant paradigm shift. I immediately re-scale the size of my worries, and feel gratitude for the things in my life that are going so well, and relief that the car crash did not affect my family or those I love.

International Reframe

Several years ago I was doing a solo concert tour of Chile, South America. I was playing a concert in the southernmost city in the world, Punta Arenas. I happened to have a free day before the concert, and as I was acting as an ambassador of the Canadian Government on that trip, the governmental officials of Chile wished to show me the area. With a full 72 hours before the concert, I agreed, though I wanted to be sure to return from any trip in time to practice for the concert which included some very difficult pieces.

Early the next morning we left Punta Arenas and traveled by jeep to Tierra Del Fuego. This is an incredible and fascinating part of the world, where huge rocks and ice jut straight out of the sea and the mixture of gray ocean and desolate coastline is awe-inspiring. It was the middle of August, which is winter in Chile. The roads were in terrible condition and wound around the mountains with steep cliffs on one side and a hundred-foot gorge on the other. Three men accompanied me: the representative of the Chilean government, a driver and a translator. Unfortunately, about six hours away from civilization, the jeep got horribly stuck. Though we tried for hours, with all of us pushing and tugging in the ice and snow, we could not manage to push the jeep out. To make things worse, nightfall was approaching. There was no radio in the jeep and we were more than 100 miles from any human settlement. And it was cold!

Within walking distance, we found a very small shack that was used by the forestry service. It had no provisions, but there was a fireplace and we found some wood to make a fire. After a while it became evident that there was nothing to do but lie down on the cold floor and try to sleep. In the middle of the night, I awoke with a feeling of terror. The three men accompanying me were all asleep, but a log from the fire had rolled out onto the floor of the shack and was smoldering. The whole shack was thick with smoke, so that it was almost impossible to breathe. I woke all the men and we crawled to the door and faced a cold, Chilean night, huddled together for warmth. Had I not awoken, we all would have died of smoke inhalation. The next morning the embassy sent out a search party and we were transported back to Punta Arenas, arriving at the concert hall fifteen minutes before the concert was to begin. Fortunately, the government officials had moved my harp and my suitcases to the concert hall, hoping that I would be found in time to perform.

Talk about a paradigm shift! Any thought of worrying about knowing the music went out the window. I quickly changed backstage, combing the smoke and soot out of my hair. I remember vividly my emotions on stage that night, incredibly thankful to be alive and able to play the music I so loved. I proceeded to play one of the best concerts of my life. The paradigm shift from first being fearful of missing a note to being fearful for my life has never left me, and I now try to refocus and view my nervousness in a bigger, more realistic, paradigm.

Have you ever been so concerned with an upcoming event or challenge that everything else got completely out of perspective? I recommend that you remember the power of shifting the paradigm of your concern. Reframing techniques from the preceding chapter are an invaluable tool in re-establishing perspective. Another wonderful tool is called the Circle of Influence.

Circle of Influence

Back in vaudeville days, the famous Marx Brothers comedy team used to travel by train from town to town, playing a different Vaudeville theatre every night. The brothers did not have a guaranteed fee for the evening. Instead, they received a percentage of any money made at the door. In these days, their mother used to accompany the brothers on tour. Every night she would sit at the side of the stage, peering out of the curtain as the audience came in. She would become totally panicked that

138

not enough people would come to the concert so that the Marx Brothers could afford the railway tickets to the next town and the next performance. They called this worrying, "Flop sweat." What was unique about Flop sweat was that no matter how much worrying Mrs. Marx did, and no matter how agitated she became backstage, there was absolutely nothing she could do to help the situation. It was out of her control, or her "Circle of Influence." On the other hand, the four Marx Brothers who were touring at that time had done a brilliant thing in assigning this concern to their mother. Since she was having the Flop sweat, the brothers were free to concentrate only on their performance.

Do you ever find yourself in a situation where you have a task to do, such as a performance, but you can see that the people who are supposed to be setting things up for you *aren't doing it right?* The lighting isn't right, the podium is in the wrong place, the chairs are being set up too far forward, etc. Instinctively, you want to move the podium and make the changes yourself so that everything is perfect. But changing the lighting is not really something you have control over.

It is important to separate those things that you can change, and are appropriate for you to worry about, and those that you do not have control over. For example, you can control how early you arrive at the theatre, and how prepared you are. You cannot control the audience size or what the critic might write. Learning to clearly differentiate between these two categories is to have a clear grasp on what is within your *circle of influence.*

Circle of Influence refers to deciding *exactly what things you have direct control over, and which things* (like how many people came to the Marx Brothers shows) *are totally out of your control.* Imagine a circle around yourself. Inside the circle are included how you are thinking, how focused you are, and such elements as sorting the pages of your script or music, applying stage makeup if appropriate, being concerned with your clothing, etc. That is all that you need to be aware of. Outside your Circle of Influence is *everything else:* the audience, noises in the room, what people think, and virtually everything that you do not have direct and immediate control over. It is imperative that you stop worrying about anything not within your Circle of Influence. You can't control it and even if you could, it is not your job. Circle of Influence is a marvelous and freeing concept to be aware of. The value of this important tool will be determined by how strict you are with yourself in observing and honoring the concept. Let's look at a few examples of what would or would not, in certain instances, be included in your Circle of Influence.

Scene one: a speaker is asked to give an important presentation for an international conference. He includes state-of-the-art visual examples, and calls the conference planners to make sure that Power Point is available for the presentation.

- ❖ He arrives at the conference center and finds out that his speech is going to be given in a tent, outside. There is nothing that he can do about this so he accepts it as being *outside his Circle of Influence.*
- ❖ He finds out that at the same time as he is giving his speech, the governor is giving a welcoming address in another building. This will probably affect how many people will hear his (brilliant) presentation. This is definitely outside his Circle of Influence. The decision had been made already and is not negotiable. Outside his Circle of Influence is to try to change the time or

location. *Within his Circle of Influence* is his ability to alter the placing of the chairs for the audience so it looked as though he anticipated a small crowd, and so the presentation would be intimate and (he chose to believe), more effective.

❖ There was no power for the computer and his visuals, which he considered imperative to the success of the presentation. This is *under his Circle of Influence.* First he calls maintenance who say they don't have a 100-foot extension cord. (Remember, he was relegated to a tent. The extension cord had to reach from the adjoining building.) Furthermore, the security guards are concerned about running an extension cord that far, in case people trip over it. Our speaker sees that this could be remedied with an attitude of *"keep trying until something works."* He has allowed himself plenty of time before his presentation, so he is not rushed or stressed by time. He hails a cab and travels to the nearest hardware store, buying an extra-long extension cord and two rolls of heavy duct tape. Returning to the event site, he connects the power supply, tapes it down, and receives the blessings of the security people, the maintenance people, and the organizers who are ready to deal with another unhappy presenter. **This "can-do" attitude set the stage for a brilliant and inspiring presentation.**

Scene Two: You are a concert pianist and are about to do your debut performance in an important concert venue. You know the music, you have done a dress rehearsal in the hall, and you went back to your hotel to rest before the concert.

Now you are in a taxi returning to the concert hall for the performance. Unfortunately, there is a terrible traffic jam in downtown New York and the taxi you are riding in is caught in traffic, unable to move for 40 minutes. You remember the importance of Circle of Influence, and analyze your options:

- ❖ The concert hall is too far away to walk to, and no other traffic is moving, so you realize that you must remain in the cab and wait it out.
- ❖ You now have only yourself to be concerned with; in fact, how you feel about the situation is the only thing within your Circle of Influence. *You can both stress and fret, which will negatively impact the performance, or make the best use of the time you have.*
- ❖ Feeling empowered by realizing what you have control over, you calmly review your music, holding it up to reconfirm your visual memory (and also keeping kinesthetic-based panic at bay.)
- ❖ You have toiletries and mirror with you and you use the time to comb your hair, etc. to be ready to perform when you arrive.
- ❖ You use a cell phone to alert the concert hall to hold the door 15 minutes.
- ❖ Having completed all that you can do, you sit back and do deep breathing exercises and even a short meditation. Envision yourself arriving at the hall in plenty of time, confident and self-assured, loving the experience, and having a great success.

Obviously, there are as many potential scenarios as your imagination can think up, and pre-thinking as many elements as you can before the concert day is ideal. If a stressful situation arises despite your pro-active attention to detail, it is important to ask yourself, *"Have I any control over this situation? Is there anything I can change?"* If the answer is "no," then immediately direct your attention to those things that *are* within your Circle of Influence. Feel great about yourself because you are rising above the challenge, and proceed with confidence and a positive attitude. Do a Paradigm Shift, minimizing the importance of the elements you cannot alter, and proceed to give a Power Performance that you and your audience are going to remember as a huge success.

If musicians allow the environment to affect the quality of their performance, they have robbed the audience and themselves of a potentially wonderful experience. Further, it is unacceptable professional behavior to be a "prima donna." Although the public might put up with eccentric behaviors for a short while, it is a true professional who knows how to take care of business, to handle any difficulties that come along, and to not let the unexpected upset them. This is the artist that will make it in the long run, and have a much more enjoyable time along the way!

MAKIN' IT HAPPEN ... choose
3 of these ideas and put them into practice TODAY!

1. Think back to the last public appearance that you gave. Remember all of the things that happened on that day which were unexpected. Take a piece of paper and make two columns, one marked **XX** for those things you had **no** control over, and one marked **00** for those things that you did have influence over. It will be illuminating to think back about the events that caused you concern or panic, and see if perhaps some of them were in the **XX** category. Think of how much mental energy you might save in another similar situation by not allowing yourself to become involved with elements outside your Circle of Influence.

2. Search your mind for something that is a "nagging concern" or doubt. It may be associated with your profession, or with personal interactions, or with your own capabilities. Now, try a

paradigm shift, altering the way that you are viewing that problem. One marvelous question to ask yourself is, "Will this matter in ten years?" Viewing things from the future is an instant paradigm shift, and often enables us to see things in a more realistic perspective.

3. Think of an upcoming concert or public appearance that you will be giving. Visualize yourself walking through every part of the experience. Think of all the variables that might arise, and make an immediate decision in your mind if they are within your Circle of Influence. If they are things you cannot control, congratulate yourself for not wasting energy becoming agitated. For example, see yourself on stage setting up the lighting. You tell the lighting technician (up on the catwalk) that you definitely need more light to see your music or the instrument. The lighting man explains that every working light is on you right now, and there is absolutely nothing else he can do. You hear yourself say, "Great . . . then the lighting is perfect!"

4. One of the most ridiculous things that people tend to worry about is what someone else is going to do or what they may think. Talk about something outside your Circle of Influence! Catch yourself as you invest important creative energy second-guessing what someone else will do, or what they might be thinking.

There is a wonderful phrase that I first heard in a conversation between Deepak Chopra and Wayne Dyer. "Look after what is your business, and leave the details up to the universe . . . after all, the universe is going to look after the details anyway!"

–11–

YOU THE TEACHER

Access Your Own Excellence

Have you ever had someone explain a concept to you, and you immediately realized that you actually *knew* the information before? The words resounded inside you and you were in perfect harmony with the ideas being presented.

Often something that a teacher or a coach tells us will resonate with us because we already instinctively know the information on a subliminal level. The next technique, known in Neuro Linguistic Programming as "Triple Position," involves tapping into your own instinctive knowledge. **You become the Teacher**.

This technique can have a powerful impact upon your level of excellence, no matter what form of performance you are undertaking. The basis of this technique is the understanding that we all have the knowledge and potential inside us to do whatever we need to do. The trick is to learn to open yourself up and access the awesome capabilities and knowledge that you already possess.

In order to learn this exercise, you need three pieces of paper, regular 8 ½ by 11 is perfect. Make each piece of paper a different color if possible. Write on these papers in large, heavy writing the numbers 1, 2, and 3. Lay the three pieces of paper on the floor in a large triangle, with each sheet about four feet apart. It should look something like this:

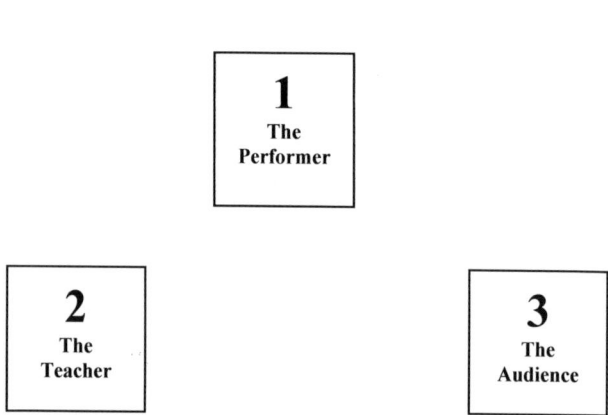

1. First, stand on sheet number 1. When you stand on this sheet, you are **the performer**. Go through all the motions (with great concentration), of performing a piece on a musical instrument, or giving a speech or reciting lines in a play. It is possible to do this without making any sound, just imagine how the performance looks, sounds, and feels. Hold your imaginary instrument in your hands and move your fingers exactly as you would in performance. If speaking, see yourself addressing an audience and hear in your mind exactly what you would say. Take breaths at appropriate points, and be aware of the timing of your presentation. The more real you can make this experience, the better. Finish out your presentation

2. Now, move to stand on sheet number two. When you are in this position, you are **the teacher.** Imagine a master

teacher, either a real person who has inspired you or a fictional person you are creating in your mind. Now become that person. As the teacher, look back at sheet number one and recall with great detail the performance that was just given. Review this performance from a master teacher's point of view, noticing anything and everything that could be improved. In your mind, communicate your suggestions for improvement back to **the performer**. Try moving back to sheet one (again becoming **the performer**) to incorporate all the changes that **the teacher** has recommended. Allow yourself to go back and forth between these two until the teacher is satisfied with the performer's presentation, and you have learned everything possible from this interaction.

3. Now, stand on sheet number three. Now you are viewing the performance as **the audience**. Replay your internal video of your performance and this time critique it from the point of view of a non-expert member of your audience. Notice how the **audience** member is concerned about different things than the **teacher** is: for a violinist, the teacher may see that you are carrying a lot of stress in your bow arm, whereas the audience member is concerned that you frown and chew your lip when you play difficult passages. Review the whole performance from the position of the audience, and then make any suggestions for improvement to the performer. Often the performer realizes that their performance was more successful than they thought, especially when viewed from **the audience**.

When you are finished with the whole exercise, gather the papers and save them to use another time, or to use with students. You will probably feel amazed at what you were able to teach yourself. Realize that this insight is yours to learn from, any time you wish.

Really Do It!

A violinist that I worked with incorporated this tool into her regular practice procedure. As she was learning a piece, she would play a section and then in her imagination step a few paces aside, and view what she had just played from a teacher's standpoint. She would immediately incorporate the suggestions, and then repeat the same procedure with a new section of her performance. This exercise is really a variation on a reframe because you are seeing yourself through different eyes. A wonderful element of this type of practicing is that there is immediacy to making the changes, so that bad habits do not have time to establish themselves. You are allowing yourself to correct and hone your art as it is being developed, working on your product *as it is at this moment.* The advantages of this are many. We cannot correct what we cannot see . . . and this allows you to see and hear any shortcomings or problems from three separate vantage points.

I often play "You the Teacher" when I am on concert tours, using my time effectively when I am on long plane flights. I find it is not necessary to actually step onto the three pieces of paper. Instead I can just mentally shift positions so that I am the performer, the master teacher or the audience, and reap the benefits of the exercise while I am stuck in transit.

What Others Think and How Important is It Anyway

Since I was a tiny child, I dreamt about becoming a famous harpist. In my mind, the highest honor possible was to be invited to perform the opening recital for the American Harp Society. This was the equivalent, for me, of *really making it.* Since I had built this up as such a momentous event (over a period of thirty years or so), when I did receive an invitation to give this prestigious opening concert, I felt some trepidation. I would be performing in front of harpists from all over the world. What if they didn't like me? What if I made mistakes? I was investing a lot of time worrying about what my audience might think. I knew this to be very dangerous, for how can you possibly play well if half of your energy is out in the audience being judgmental? It is hard enough to play a concert with 100% of your energy, let alone dividing that in half! And yet, even if I realized intellectually that worrying what my audience would think was detrimental to my success, I continued to do it.

At the time I received the invitation to perform, I was taking an NLP training course in Los Angeles, working with an NLP practitioner named Gary Boon. He did such a wonderful reframe with me that I would like to present it to you here.

GARY: Carrol, imagine that you just played the opening concert in front of all those harpists. You were really not very happy about how it went, and didn't feel very satisfied. As you walk off stage, you are greeted by a famous harpist. She says, "Well, it was O.K. but I really didn't like your tempos in the Bach. It was much too fast, and it's not a very good piece anyway. Also you should never wear that color on stage. It did not look good from the audience. And I don't like the last piece you played." How do you feel?

CARROL: Devastated. Horrible. I want to crawl into a dark hole and hide.

GARY: Okay, let's try another scenario. First, wipe the screen in your mind completely clean. Now, see yourself playing on stage, and you love the way it is going. You are very satisfied with your performance. You are enjoying the elegance of the music and feel very in rapport with your audience. You walk off stage and the same harpist says exactly the same thing. What is your reaction?

CARROL: I don't care what she thinks! It is amazing, but all of a sudden her words have no effect on me.

GARY: Right! So, in other words, you really don't care what the audience thinks *as long as you are satisfied with yourself.* Therefore, if you center your energies and your concerns on playing *the way that pleases you,* then you rob your audience of the power to upset you with their judgments.

What is truly wonderful about this new attitude I learned, is that when I love what I am playing, and when I am pleased with my performance, the audience always joins me – they love it too! How much easier it is to play for my own approval, rather that dividing my energies and my confidence by trying to second-guess what someone else will think.

As for the opening recital for the harpists, I loved it and remember thinking after the second piece, "Hey, this is fun! I am really enjoying myself." It was a high point of my career, and one that I would not change at all, even if I had the power to do so.

Design an Audience

Have you ever had the experience of feeling like you were divided on stage? Part of you is performing and another part is trying to mind-read whether the audience likes you.

If you do have a tendency to let your mind wander out to your audience, wondering what they think, try the following technique which I developed when I was on a very arduous concert tour, and had performances every night. I found the more exhausted I became, the more I was bothered by anxiety about my performance. As I moved into more prestigious concert halls in New York and Washington, it seemed the "stakes went up," and I felt I needed to play even more perfectly for those sophisticated audiences.

One night backstage I had a talk with myself before the performance. I realized that I was feeling like a trespasser on alien territory . . . that the audience that was going to hear me that night was not my friend and supporter, but somehow on the opposing team. (To those of you who have ever had conversations with yourself, you know that logic is not an important element in such discussions.)

Ask yourself, "Who could I perform for who would absolutely love everything they heard?" The answer for me was instantaneous. It was my young daughter. So, I decided to – in my mind – take my daughter on stage with me and play for her. I visualized an image of my daughter and then, in my mind, shrank her down to about two inches high. As I walked on stage that night, I took "my daughter" out with me and, in my mind, sat her on the base of my harp. As I played each piece, I dedicated it to her gentle, appreciative, loving image. What a great time I had! I found that I was extraordinarily focused and played without stress.

Many years later, I sometimes find myself in a situation where focus is a challenge. It might be that someone in the audience is making noise, or I have just seen a famous harpist in the first row, or anything that distracts my normal concentration. Even in the middle of a piece, I can envision my daughter listening to my harp and if I channel my attention to concentrate on performing for her, I can regain my focus and eliminate any distractedness I may have been experiencing. I alter my awareness and focus on one thing, which is to perform for someone who accepts and loves me without condition.

This focusing technique is similar to what often happens in meditation. By channeling your thoughts to one image, you are drawing all your concentration together and allowing yourself to focus. The advantage is that all of this can happen in a couple of seconds, and your audience will never be aware that anything happened, except that the performance became more intense and confident.

The Bubble

This technique is especially successful if you have a team of players or an ensemble. Have the group stand around in a circle immediately before the performance. Imagine that there is a huge vat of magic bubble liquid in the center of the group. Each person holds an imaginary bubble wand (the same as a child would play with). On the count of three, everyone dips their wands into the brew and then raises their arms, collectively creating a bubble around the whole group. This bubble has very special powers, and will remain around all of you all the time you are on stage. The magic of the bubble is that any wrong notes or mistakes that any member of the group might make, will simply go to the edge of the bubble, then bounce off and fall back into the bubble, therefore not being discernable to the audience. Similarly, any negative thoughts or energy that the audience might feel will bounce off the other side of the bubble, and not be felt by you on stage. Only the right notes and loving, supportive energy can permeate this bubble. Since wrong notes won't be heard by the audience, you will be less concerned with them and they probably won't even happen.

Green Light

The athletic department at the University of Arizona has a resident "mental coach." His name is Jeff Jenssen, author of *Winning the Mental Game*. Jeff designed an anchoring technique which is highly effective with sports teams that he coaches. I have found it to be a positive element in establishing an ideal performance state for performers in all venues.

He uses the image of a traffic signal, with green, yellow and red lights. If you are "in the red," you are experiencing self-doubt and inhibition. By accessing past successes and using the reframing techniques such as those presented in earlier chapters, it is possible to change your state of mind from a red zone into yellow, and finally to green, where you are confident and ready to perform at your best.

In Jeff's approach to sports, a batter going up to the plate, for example, determines what space he is in and does not make his final approach until he feels he is "in the green." To anchor this in with a visual reminder, Jeff uses small green stickers, which he puts on the ends of the bats. When the player sees the green sticker, he is reminded that he must force his mind into its most positive posture, in order to play his best.

After my students worked with Jeff, I put a small green sticker high up on the crown of the harp for their final performances of the semester. This proved very successful. My students saw the green stickers which reminded them that they needed to concentrate, focus, and celebrate their own highest achievements. In addition, because the stickers were placed high on the instruments, this necessitated the students looking up, causing each person to begin their performance in visual mode. They were exceptionally fine performances! Put a green sticker on your own script or music and anchor in memories of fabulous performances you have given.

MAKIN' IT HAPPEN ...choose
3 of these ideas and put them into practice TODAY!

1. Sit down and make yourself a list of as many positive attributes as you can about   yourself. Divide this into categories as follows:

    1. Things that I am good at
    2. Compliments I have received from people I value (like coaches, teachers, etc.)
    3. My achievements (degrees, concerts, awards)

    Recall this list when you want to put yourself into the "green zone" for maximum performance. This is also a great list to "anchor in" as discussed in Chapter Eight.

2. Think of a person who views what you do with total acceptance, someone who really believes in you and applauds all your achievements without criticism. Now, imagine that you can shrink that person small enough to take on stage with you . . . or into any challenging environment. As you give your presentation, be confident that you are being received with open arms and that your audience is totally in rapport with you as you mentally perform for this miniature person, your strongest supporter.

3. Think of a time coming up when you can use "You The Teacher." Instead of standing on three pieces of paper, you might decide upon three different vantage points in a room, such as by the wall (performer), sitting on a chair beside the performer,

(teacher) and standing in the middle of the room, (audience.) Perhaps you might even want to try this out on a concert stage, where you mentally perform from center stage, listen from stage right and critique as an audience from the center of the hall. Make sure that as you do your performance you give it total concentration and commitment. "Be" the teacher, and then the audience, and immediately incorporate their suggestions into your performance.

4. Sit at your instrument and perform a piece, or stand before a microphone and recite your speech or introduction. Following that real-life performance, analyze what you just did from the position of the coach (teacher) and from your audience.

5. See yourself doing "the bubble" at an upcoming performance. Imagine that you have a cauldron of magic bubble solution in front of you, and you are going to put your bubble wand down into the liquid and draw it up and over your head to engulf yourself in this protective covering. As you perform from within this ephemeral sphere, you are reminded that music is a highly refined form of communication. Compared to the importance of communicating your joy and enthusiasm for your art, "wrong notes" are really very immaterial anyway. Just ask your imaginary audience, from exercise three. They probably didn't even know there were any mistakes!

–12–

IN THE FINAL ANALYSIS

When It Doesn't Work

In this book we have been examining many different methods and tools to ensure that you have positive experiences when performing in front of other people. However, it would be naïve to think that you will always experience only success in performance.

When a performance does not go well, it can be very disheartening. No matter what the situation was, one thing is certain; that when you did your performance, you were giving it your best. Every part of your body and mind was trying to have a successful experience.

There can actually be as much value to you from a "bad" performance as from a successful one. You can learn a lot by thinking back over the circumstances that preceded your less-than-ideal performance and deciding what to alter in the future. Consider the following:

❖ Did you start your preparations early enough? (Probably not!) If you didn't, what an invaluable learning experience for you! Next time, increase your preparation time by at least 50%. The whole experience will be so much easier and less stressful.

157

❖ If you did allow yourself enough time, were you conscientious in maintaining practice on the project consistently, daily? Think about tools presented in this book that might assist you to be more diligent the next time around.

❖ Did you do ten pre-performances? How about five? *None?* Shame on you. No excuses. Change this next time. Set up at least five pre-performances the minute you accept your next performance. Consider how much better you would feel now if the performance you just gave were only a practice and not the real thing.

❖ In front of the public, did you allow internal conversation and nerves to take over? If so, re-read chapters five and six, and make sure to do all the exercises in **MAKIN' IT HAPPEN**.

Okay, so you know what you didn't do, and that undoubtedly had a negative impact on your success on stage. The fact remains that you are still carrying around the result of a negative experience in front of the public. This is dangerous and tiring, for as long as the memory of that perceived failure remains lurking around inside your mind, you will always harbor a fear that it might happen again. Although fear of failure can be a motivator to practice, an intense negative experience does far more harm than good, so it is time to lose that memory and all of the self-doubt that is associated with it.

The Power of Disassociation

Disassociation is a very effective tool for many people. It often has an immeasurably positive, even life changing, impact. This exercise is much more effective when it is done with two people. I will describe it here as if you have a friend to assist you. In fact, if you found a partner with whom you could do many of these Power Performance techniques, you would both benefit greatly. While this technique is most effective when done with another person, there is still a great deal of value in doing it by yourself if no one else if available. Originally called a "Phobia Cure" in LNP, this technique is a variation on "You The Teacher."

Begin by carefully looking back into your memory bank. Find a situation that is not resolved and still carries has associated anxiety and stress. The first time I did this, I remembered a performance in South America that still upset me. Every time I thought of that performance I experienced rocks in my stomach, dragging me down and annihilating any positive energy I had. I had carried this image with me for almost 20 years, and the weight of that memory, even after the passage of many years, still took a toll on my self-confidence.

It was at the hands of the great Performance Excellence and NLP master, my dear friend and mentor Michael Colgrass, that this demon was purged from my psyche. I urge you to read through the following directions and then find a friend or colleague to do this exercise with. One of the things to remember is that the person who is assisting you with this never becomes aware of the content of the problem that you are dealing with. You get to keep the content of your experience to yourself. The other person only serves as a facilitator in the process.

Your Turn

Here is the procedure I experienced. Perform the steps of this technique with a friend or colleague. I have put comments in italics to assist you when you do this exercise with a friend.

MICHAEL sat opposite CARROL, close enough so that he could reach out and easily touch her knee. MICHAEL was the facilitator.

CARROL recalls a memory from her past that is not serving her, the performance in South America. She really wanted to alter the effect that the memory of that performance has on her, to "purge" the negative energy.

MICHAEL: "Please close your eyes and relax. Bring to your mind a situation or event from your past that is troublesome. Relive that experience in its entirety. Use all of your senses as you recall this scene. Remember how the air felt, and the texture of your clothes against your skin. Recall if you felt warm or cold, and if there were any smells associated with the scene. Recall any sounds that were present, and hear clearly all that transpired. See with vivid detail all of the people involved in this picture and recall where they were in relation to you. Be *in that picture.* Relive it from your memory with the intensity and clarity of the first time it happened. I want you to be yourself, in this situation, doing exactly what you did, and feeling the same feelings. When you have finished, let me know by nodding your head. You may keep your eyes closed."

Note: It is not important to say exactly these words. The main thing is to get the person to access the memory as vividly as possible. At this point the facilitator will probably see visual signs that the client is re-experiencing the event. Often their breathing will become shallower and there will be changes in the person's physiology, especially in face color. Do not be concerned if the person expresses feelings by sighing, crying, or moving to and fro. This is simply an indication that they are completely reliving the experience, and are re-experiencing the discomfort and pain associated with it.

MICHAEL: "Now see the same scene happening on a large stage. See the whole scene again, with you in the center of the stage. We will call this image **You on Stage.** *Note: As you say, "You on Stage." gently tap the person's knee. This adds an important kinesthetic anchor to the experience.*

MICHAEL: Nod when you are finished viewing it.

CARROL: recalls the experience (ouch!) and nods.

MICHAEL: Now I want you to replay the same scene, on the stage, but this time I want you to imagine that you are viewing the whole scene **as if you were sitting out in the audience viewing everything that happened.** Go ahead. When you are finished, nod your head. You are **In the Audience.** *(tap as you say, "The Audience.")*

CARROL: *nods.*

MICHAEL: Now, view it again from **You on Stage.** *(tap as you say "You on Stage." You are going to implant this kinesthetic anchor every time you have the person's perspective change. Gradually you will speed up the time between your comments, eventually allowing them to only experience a part of the original scene.)*

MICHAEL: Now be **The Audience** (tap) and view it again.

MICHAEL: Now, I want you to view yourself doing exactly the same thing, but this time you are seeing it from way up in the **Balcony.** Play the whole scene in your mind, viewing it from the **Balcony.** *(tap as you say " Balcony." Every time you say, "On Stage, Audience, or Balcony," you tap.)*

MICHAEL: Now be **You on Stage.** *(tap)*
                   Balcony *(tap)*
                   Audience *(tap)*
                   Balcony *(tap)*
                   You on stage *(tap)*
                   Audience *(tap)*
                   You on stage *(tap)*
                   Balcony *(tap)*

Note: there is no need to follow this script exactly! Simply jump back and forth between the three positions at your discretion. As you do this, decrease the time between each statement, going faster and faster between the three options. Do not give them time to view the whole sequence, just enough time to establish the picture. The speed of changing between You on Stage, Audience and Balcony should increase until the person is experiencing several vantage points per second. You are aiming at disassociating any residual feelings that the person has associated with the scene, so you are aiming at putting them "off balance."

MICHAEL: "Okay, terrific job. By the way, did you see the news this morning? *(Or any other question that completely changes the subject, such as, "Do you have a cat or dog?")* After a few minutes of conversation on different topics, ask the person to recall the original image and assess for you how they now feel about it. In almost all cases, the anxiety of the original picture will be drastically reduced and the person will be free of the feeling of dread and depression that they originally associated with the memory.

When I did this exercise, seeing my performance from the audience's perspective was especially illuminating. When I viewed my own performance from the audience's perspective, I couldn't even find the mistakes I thought I had made! When I viewed it from the balcony, not only could I not find any mistakes, but also I was pretty impressed with how the whole thing came off. By the time I had whirled these three images together, I felt like I could let that memory go, and go on to achieving other things. The sinking sensation I always felt when I thought of that performance was gone, and I felt ready to face other challenges. The next time I played that piece, I knew I could "ace" it and be full of self-confidence.

Suppose that you don't have another person with whom you can do this exercise. It is possible to sit quietly and recall a performance or situation that was stressful for you, and basically to go through the above steps. According to your individual makeup, the physical anchor may or may not be a part of the exercise you want to do for yourself. A particularly auditory person might want to hear in their mind a loud obnoxious buzzing sound when they need to make the adjustment and see the scene from another perspective. A highly visual person might choose to see an incredibly bright flash of light as they change the scenes.

After you finish the exercise, I recommend a little "tidying up" of the loose ends. Take any residual feelings left regarding the scene you were working on, and make a ball out of them in your hand and toss them off into the sky (Toss It.) Or go out and bury the residual feelings, or use any of the reframing techniques from chapter Eight. After you are all finished, congratulate yourself on the hard work you have done. What a wonderful present you have given yourself. You are now rid of that heavy rock that you have been carrying in your psyche. BRAVO!

MAKIN' IT HAPPEN ... choose
3 of these ideas and put them into practice TODAY!

1. Do the disassociation exercise from this chapter. To set it up, talk to some friends who are involved in your field. Bring up the subject of Power Performance and ask if someone who has not read this book would be interested in trying some valuable techniques out with you. A wonderful phrase to use is, "It's just a game, no big deal, just something fun to explore." This way, their subconscious is not on *defense*, it is open and ready to play the game without constraint. Being relaxed about these exercises certainly does not diminish their value, and in fact the benefits will be enhanced if you view this homework as a joy and not a difficult task.

2. Take a piece of paper and list for yourself all the Power Performance tools that you can use to clear your mind of debris, thus setting the stage for many Power Performances. Skim back through the book if you choose, to remind yourself of all the techniques. Now add a couple of your own ideas. Take a red pen and circle *three* techniques that appeal to you most. They may be ones which you have done at the end of other chapters, or they may be new ideas you have not tried yet. Now, write these three techniques down on a small piece of paper, which you are going to put up on your fridge, or the mirror in your bathroom. For the next three days, commit to trying one technique per day. If you find one that feels particularly comfortable for you, use that tool often enough for it to become a habit.

3. The next time a colleague, student or family member comes to you to talk about   something that is upsetting to them, do the above exercise together. In this case, frame it as "Do you want to play a game? Just do what I ask you. Doesn't matter if it works or not, let's just explore what happens." Now proceed with the

technique. Don't explain it, just do it. You may find that doing it "just for fun" is even more effective than doing it with someone who is aware of the technique and Power Performance concepts and is using a portion of his or her mind (even if they don't intend to) to analyze what is happening.

CONCLUSION

"I just opened the door . . . "

The day after I received my Master of Music Degree from the Juilliard School in New York, the Government of Canada (I am Canadian) awarded me a very special honor. They paid all the expenses for me to give a debut recital in Carnegie Hall. This is every musician's dream, and to have the government believe in you enough to pay for it was truly spectacular.

Everything went wonderfully that night. I loved how I played. I actually remember ending my first piece and thinking to myself, "I am having fun! I don't think you are supposed to have fun in a New York Debut." But I did have fun and, gratefully, so did the audience. Later that evening, after the champagne reception and amidst a myriad of gorgeous floral presentation bouquets, my family attempted to thank the Minister of Culture for the Province of Alberta who had come from Canada for the concert. In response to our "Thank you SO MUCH" the Minister had the following response:

"We just opened the door. It is YOU who went through the door, and took advantage of the opportunities that were presented. It is YOU who deserves the credit for maximizing the benefit of anything we have provided."

That would summarize my hope for the information in this book. Look at the techniques, tools, and performing insights presented here as doors that you can go through at your own speed and comfort level, to discover a new and magical world of successful, enjoyable and rewarding performing experiences. Just like practicing, it is important to use these skills often. Repeating them until they are a habit multiplies the benefit to you.

Remember always that you are the best example of YOU that exists. And you are a work of art in progress. Celebrate your individuality, and be proud of your many accomplishments.

What really matters is that you are continually trying to hone your skills, to communicate more successfully with any audience, and to master your art. Celebrate every opportunity to overcome the challenges of every situation, and have fun experiencing the empowering joy of **Power Performance**.

For additional books, music and recordings, and information about Dr. Carrol's workshops and seminars, visit our website:

www.integrityink.us

2063579

Made in the USA